Fashion in the French Revolution

Aileen Ribeiro

Fashion in the French Revolution

Holmes & Meier Publishers, Inc., New York

Library of Congress Cataloging-in-Publication Data

Ribeiro, Aileen, 1944–
    Fashion in the French Revolution.
    (Costume & civilization)
    Bibliography: p.
    Includes index.
    1. Costume—France—History—Revolution, 1789–1799.
2. France—Social life and customs—1789–1815.
I. Title. II. Series.
GT867.R53 1988 391′.00944 88-21242
ISBN 0-8419-1197-5 (alk. paper)

Typeset by Latimer Trend & Company Ltd, Plymouth
and printed in Great Britain

Contents

Acknowledgements

Ever since I published a book entitled *Dress in Eighteenth-Century Europe 1715–1789*, in 1984, I have had a sequel in mind which would concentrate on the French Revolution, that event which marked the end of the eighteenth century in so many ways. Over the last few years I have had the opportunity to examine a number of collections – of fine and applied arts, including costume and textiles, printed material, rare books, etc. – both in this country and abroad, which relate to the vast topic of the French Revolution; in no way can I claim here to have done anything more than a preliminary study of what is a most complex subject.

I owe a debt to the many libraries, museums and art galleries listed in this book, both for their help and advice in matters of research, and for providing photographs of items in their collections.

My greatest debt is to the Courtauld Institute; staff from the book and Witt Libraries were particularly helpful, and the Photographic Department provided a large number of photo

graphs. I would like to thank the Prints and Drawings departments of the British Museum and the Victoria & Albert Museum; also the British Library. In Paris I must thank the staff of the Archives Nationales, the Bibliothèque Nationale, the Bibliothèque Historique de la Ville de Paris, and the Bibliothèque d'Art et d'Archéologie of the University of Paris (Fondation Jacques Doucet).

I would like to thank the British Academy for a research grant enabling me to visit a number of museums and libraries in the United States, in particular the comprehensive collections held by the Library of Congress.

Finally I would like to mention a few names. Firstly to thank Alice Mackrell and Jennifer Harris, both of whom have worked on dress during the French Revolution, and to whom I am obviously indebted. Then I would like to record my gratitude for his interest and encouragement, to Robert Ribeiro. Last, but not least, I would like to thank Rachel Wright at Batsford for her wise editorial advice.

Illustrations

Jacket illustrations:

Front: *Le Triomphe de Marat 1794* (detail)
Louis-Léopold Boilly
Oil on canvas
Musée des Beaux-Arts, Lille

Back: *Portrait of a Woman, c.* 1794–5
Circle of David
Oil on canvas
San Diego Museum of Art

Colour plates

Chronological table 1789–1799

'Histoire complète de la Révolution'

Vive la nation! vive la liberté! vive le tiers-état! à bas les aristocrates! vive d'Orléans! vive la Fayette! vive Necker! vive Mirabeau! vive le roi! vive notre bon roi! vive le restaurateur de la liberté! vive la constitution de 91! à bas les républicains du champ de Mars! Pétion[1] ou la mort! vive la mort! à bas la monarchie et vive le 10 août! vive Robespierre! vive Marat! vive Danton! vivent Tallien[2] et le 2 septembre! vive la république! vive les jacobins, vive la montagne! à bas les églises, et pas de bon dieu! vive le gouvernement révolutionnaire! vive la terreur! vive le maximum! vive l'Être Suprême! et l'immortalité de l'âme, donc! vive la constitution de 93! vive Barère![3] vive Collot!-[4] vive Couthon![5] vive Saint-Just![6] vive le comité sauveur! vive la guillotine! périssent les conspirateurs!

. . . Ah! ah! ah! ah! vive le 9 thermidor! vivent les modérés! à bas les jacobins! mort aux assassins du peuple! vive l'humanité et la justice! le roi et du pain! du pain, citoyens représentans, du pain! vive la constitution de 95! à bas les réélections! point de cinq-cents! à bas les cinq-cents! vivent les cinq-cents! à bas le directoire qui replace tous les terroristes! vive le directoire qui épure . . . Vivent l'argent et les principes.'

Feuilleton de Littérature, Spectacles, Anecdotes, Modes et Avis Divers 9 Prairial An VI (29 May 1798)

1. Jerome Pétion, elected Mayor of Paris 14 November 1791; voted for the death of the king; proscribed with the Girondins 1793.
2. Jean-Lambert Tallien, accredited with the 1792 September massacres; later, one of the Convention leaders who helped to overthrow Robespierre on 9 Thermidor.
3. Bertrand Barère.
4. J.-M. Collot d'Herbois.
5. Georges Couthon.
6. Louis Antoine de Saint-Just.

3 to 6 were extreme Jacobins, members of the Committee of Public Safety; Couthon and Saint-Just were executed with Robespierre the day after 9 Thermidor. Collot and Barère were sentenced to deportation as a result of the popular insurrections of Germinal and Prairial 1795 against the Convention.

1789 5 May: Meeting of Estates General.
17 June: National Assembly.
20 June: Tennis Court Oath.
14 July: Storming of the Bastille.
4 August: Abolition of feudal privileges.
26 August: Declaration of the Rights of Man.
5 October: Women's march on Versailles.
6 October: Return of the royal family to Paris.
2 November: Mirabeau proposes nationalization of Church property.

1790 13 February: Suppression of religious orders.
12 July: Civil Constitution of the Clergy.
14 July: Fête de la Fédération.

1791 21 June: Flight to Varennes.
17 July: Massacre of the Champ de Mars.
27 August: Declaration of Pillnitz.
1 October: Legislative Assembly.

1792 20 April: France declares war on Austria and Prussia.
20 June: Louis wears the *bonnet rouge*.
25 July: Duke of Brunswick threatens destruction of Paris in *Manifesto of Coblentz*.
10 August: Attack on the Tuileries.
2–6 September: September massacres.
20 September: Battle of Valmy.
20 September: National Convention.
21 September: Abolition of the monarchy.
25 October: French émigrés banished for life.
6 November: Battle of Jemappes.
19 November: Declaration of assistance to all peoples wishing to throw off their government.

1793 21 January: Execution of Louis XVI.
1 February: France declares war on Britain. First Coalition v. France.
10 March: Revolutionary Tribunal in Paris.
11 March: Rising in the Vendée.
6 April: Committee of Public Safety.
31 May: Girondins overthrown.
13 July: Assassination of Marat by Charlotte Corday.
23 July: Allies drive French out of Germany.
28 July: Robespierre enters the Committee of Public Safety.
23 August: *Levée en masse*.
17 September: Law of Suspects.
29 September: Law of the General Maximum.

5 October: New calendar established.

16 October: Execution of Marie-Antoinette.

6 November: Execution of Philippe-Egalité.

4 December: Power centralized in the hands of the Committee of Public Safety, the Committee of General Security, and the Revolutionary Tribunal.

1794 24 March: Execution of the *Hébertistes* and the *Enragés*.

5–6 April: Execution of Danton and Desmoulins.

8 June: Festival of the Supreme Being.

26 June: Battle of Fleurus.

27 July (9 Thermidor): Overthrow of Robespierre.

12 November: Jacobin club of Paris closed.

8 December: Girondins re-admitted to the Convention.

24 December: Abolition of the Maximum.

1795 27 January: Batavian Republic (Netherlands).

21 February: Freedom of worship restored. Separation of Church and State.

5 April: Prussia cedes Rhine frontier.

1 April: (12 Germinal)   ⎫
                                          ⎬ Uprisings against the Convention.
20 May: (1 Prairial)   ⎭

9 June: Death of the Dauphin. Comte de Provence proclaims himself Louis XVIII.

21 July: Battle of Quiberon Bay.

1 October: Annexation of Belgium.

5 October: Attack on Convention by 'reactionary' elements dispersed by Napoleon with 'a whiff of grapeshot'.

26 October: General amnesty for political detainees.

3 November: Directory.

1796 9 March: Napoleon marries Josephine Beauharnais.

11 March: Departure of Napoleon in command of the army to Italy.

10 May: Battle of Lodi.

15 May: Savoy and Nice ceded to France.

16 October: Cispadane Republic (Bologna).

15–17 November: Battle of Arcole.

1797 14 January: Battle of Rivoli.

2 February: Fall of Mantua.

14 February: Battle of Cape St Vincent.

6 June: Ligurian Republic (Genoa).

9 July: Cisalpine Republic (Lombardy).

4 September: Directory suppresses counter-revolutionary elements.

17 October: Treaty of Campo Formio – Lombardy and Belgium ceded to France.

1798   24 January: Lemanic Republic (Geneva).

15 February: Roman Republic.

9 March: France annexes left bank of Rhine.

29 March: Helvetic Republic.

11 May: Directory annuls elections which had returned too many Jacobins.

19 May: Departure of Egyptian expedition.

21 July: Battle of the Pyramids.

1 August: Battle of the Nile.

1799   26 January: Parthenopaean Republic (Naples).

19 March: Napoleon reaches Acre. August: Collapse of Franco–Italian Republics.

5 August: Beginning of royalist insurrection in South-West France.

9 October: Napoleon lands at Fréjus.

9 November: (18 Brumaire) Coup d'état ends Directory.

15 December: Consulate.

I | The Waiting Years

With the French Revolution, a period of immense political and social upheaval, we begin the modern world. In our attitudes towards ideas of freedom, of self-expression, and to the role of the state in society, we acknowledge the debt we owe to the dramatic events of 1789 and the turbulent years which followed. These are years, brief in number, which encompass the heights of political and social idealism, and the depths of misery, brutality and terror − truly the best of times, the worst of times.

The eighteenth century, pragmatic in its approach to politics and with a seemingly immutable, static society, virtually ends with the French Revolution. Already in the 1780s, however, disturbing ideas of political and social reform were in the air, fostered by the works of the *philosophes*; doubts about the obvious imperfections of contemporary political systems were mixed with the excitement of new political theories, to produce an infectious climate of optimism and a desire to put abstract ideas into practice. In the 1780s, too, we begin to see the loss of what was universally recognized as perfect taste in the arts, including dress; the eighteenth-century confidence − some might say smugness − in its uniformity of aesthetic beliefs, was to disappear under the disintegrating forces of the Revolution. With the French Revolution came for the first time, intrusive politics, a greater awareness of class differences, and a restless need for change and for self-expression − all ideas which were to be reflected in dress, that most sensitive of social barometers. This book will explore the ways in which social and political trends were reflected in dress, during the important transitional decade of the 1780s, during the years of the Revolution itself, and during the later 1790s when the Directory tried to provide a stable and fairly liberal form of government without dictatorship, only to fall victim at the end of 1799 to the ambitions of Napoleon Bonaparte.

From the very beginning, the French Revolution seemed momentous to those living through it. To Edmund Burke in his *Reflections on the Revolution in France* (1790), the Revolution would 'sweep the earth with its hurricane'. Two years later, the political journalist William Augustus Miles, who had lived in France since 1783 wrote:

The French Revolution, like the shock of a tremendous earthquake, has been felt from one extremity of the globe to the other. It has opened to the intellectual world a new train of ideas, not less bold and hazardous than novel and extraordinary, and which must eventually produce throughout the vast continent of Europe an entire change in the manners, opinions and customs of men.[1]

Burke's *Reflections* was one of the earliest hostile reactions to the Revolution. He deplored the violent pace of events, the attacks on the sanctity of property and on tradition, which he thought presaged the dissolution of the fabric of society, with the outbreak of the 'swinish multitude'; more ominously, he noted that the abstract ideal of the 'Popular Will', under the name of Liberty, might lead to tyranny. His apologia for the French court produced Tom Paine's famous comment in *The Rights of Man* (1791), that 'He pities the plumage, but forgets the dying bird'; rather more prosaically, Miles, while feeling sorrow for 'insulted and degraded majesty', felt that Burke should have regard for 'the suffering of millions'. At first, the Revolution released a great amount of positive feeling in England. It was welcomed by those of all classes with democratic views, from the nobility to middle-class radicals, and among artisans and craftsmen; 'constitutional' societies were set up to agitate for political reform, and poets, artists and writers demonstrated their sympathy with the ideals of freedom which the early events of the Revolution seemed to embody.

However, admiration gave way during 1792 to worry, fear and horror, when the French royal family were imprisoned; after the events of 10 August, the only Englishmen who were welcome in Paris were radicals, like Paine, who had been elected as honorary republicans to the Convention. After the execution of Louis XVI in January 1793 and the subsequent declaration of war, Paris was closed to the English; the Terror of 1793–4 further alienated most English opinion, as did the expansionist ambitions of the new French republic, carried out by her invading armies.

It proved, however, impossible to prevent the spread of Jacobin ideas throughout Europe, although such an infection could, outside France, be more or less restricted. Within France, the fabric of life was immeasurably altered by the Revolution; the American historian of the Jacobins puts it well:

The guillotine, prison, Jacobin clubs, political elections, even political riots – these might all be avoided, especially by the obscure; but no one could altogether avoid clothes, theaters, furniture, cafés, games, newspapers, streets, public ceremonies, birth, death and marriage. On all this, the Revolution, and especially the Terror, left a mark. It broke in rudely on the accepted ways of millions of humble people, turned their private lives inside out, made them take part in a public life keyed to an amazing pitch of collective activity.[2]

Part of this public life revolved around the war of propaganda waged by the revolutionaries; much of it relied on visual images created by the artists who came to the support of the Revolution. These were, on the whole, the majority, for they were mainly middle class, ranked as intellectuals, and with a greater social mobility than most; even if their views were not totally in line with those of the authorities, they enjoyed relative immunity, for their work produced international fame, and was essential in promoting the ideas of the government.[3] Art was to be increasingly brought into play as an ideological tool, to be socially and politically significant; the leading figure was Jacques-Louis David, who not only painted great icon-like works exalting the heroes and martyrs of the Revolution, but also designed the great revolutionary fêtes ordered by the government, as well as a range of civil and official costume for a new, republican world.

David was not alone in his view that dress, as one of the most obvious and powerful means of communication, was worth considering in the heightened circumstances of revolutionary times. In a society full of febrile excitement, like that of Paris in the summer of 1789, fashion magazines were quick to exploit the links between fast-moving political events and costume; political allegiance as demonstrated in dress, makes fascinating reading in the pages of such periodicals as the *Magasin des Modes Nouvelles*.

The connections between fashion, politics and society were not new phenomena produced by the Revolution; costume, says the historian Ferdinand Braudel, is not just pure anecdote, 'a trifling thing', but 'an indication of deeper phenomena – of the energies, possibilities, demands and *joie de vivre* of a given society, economy and civilization.'[4]

With new ideas in the air in the 1780s, it is perhaps slightly more than a coincidence that this decade sees the establishment of high quality fashion magazines; they were quick to pick up novel trends, to explore shifting moods, temporary fads and to educate their readers both in the latest fashions and in politics, albeit – with regard to the latter – in a somewhat simplified form. The *Gallerie des Modes* (1778–87), and the *Cabinet des Modes*, later the *Magasin des Modes Nouvelles*

The Palais Royal Garden Walk. *Promenade du Jardin du Palais Royal*

1 *The Palais Royal Garden Walk*, 1787, Louis Le Coeur.

In the 1780s the Palais Royal was the place for the most fashionable shops and diversions; a slight air of dissipation was also created by the presence of ladies of the *demi-monde* and stylish *poules de luxe*. Among the bustling crowds can be seen clerics and soberly dressed professional men, young *élégants* in striped or spotted coats, and, in the right foreground, a portly *roué* wears a slouched English round hat and top boots.

The English influence can also be seen in the costume of the most prominent female figure, in the centre foreground, in her *redingote* with large caped collar. The artist has only slightly caricatured the vast plumed and ribboned hats so typical of the 1780s.

Françaises et Anglaises[5] (1785–9) provide a wealth of material on the details of fashion and the prevailing influences on it. In the 1780s, the main trend is the contrast between the sophisticated court centred formality of French dress, and the simpler, more 'egalitarian' English styles associated with that country's greater social cohesion and relative freedom under the law.

In the early years of the Revolution, the most flourishing fashion magazine was the *Journal de la Mode et du Goût*; early issues are full of enthusiasm for the Revolution, a feeling which was to become much more muted as it became obvious that the very concept of fashion, with its aristocratic and frivolous overtones, was doomed in the increasingly harsh social climate of the new republic. From the spring of 1793 fashion magazines are silent, and do not return until the summer of 1797 – not that is, until the firm establishment of 'society', in a bourgeois republic based on property.

The key fashion magazine of the Directory is

the *Journal des Dames et des Modes*, under its great editor La Mésangère; its stylish format inspired the magazine of the same name published from 1912 to 1914:

La Mésangère is a precious monument of French history . . . One knows nothing of a society when one knows nothing of the fashions that prevailed in it. Costumes reveal customs, and the toilettes of Citizenesses Tallien and Beauharnais, for example, can help us to understand the spirit of Thermidor. The historian of the Revolution . . . who has not spent a good deal of time perusing the fashion journals, is, to my mind, extremely limited.[6]

This comment by Anatole France, with its emphasis on the revelatory nature of costume on society, echoes the viewpoint of the journalist Louis-Sébastien Mercier in the often-quoted preface to his great *Tableau de Paris*:

Je vais vous parler de Paris, non de ses édifices, de ces temples, de ses monuments, de ses curiosités . . . Je parlerai des moeurs publiques & particulières, des idées regnantes, de la situation actuelle des esprits . . .'

A poor but prolific playwright, Mercier was an inspired journalist with a crusading zeal (his sympathies were republican) and with a particular ability to conjure up not only the bustling life of Paris, but what the historian Richard Cobb calls the 'histoire des mentalités' – that is, peoples' attitudes and prejudices regarding the world at large and their own private concerns. No other work shows as much insight into the part played by dress in society in late eighteenth-century Paris; Mercier's lively prose paints a vivid picture, not just of the shops and the many fashion trades which made up a not inconsiderable part of the economy of France, but also of how people felt about their clothes, and what their significance might be. In a real sense, Paris is the focus of this book. It was the capital of France, of internationally recognized canons of taste (including fashion) and good living, and events there initiated the revolutionary struggle. 'C'est

Paris qui a fait la révolution', said Mercier, and Paris kept hold of it.

Great cities, says Braudel, are 'like electric transformers. They create tension, accelerate the pace of change and constantly recharge human life'; they are the 'watersheds of human history'.[7] Being Parisian, according to Mercier, added an extra dimension to being French, good fortune in itself; it provided the bonus of being an inhabitant of the most civilized city in Europe.[8] Not for him the notion that such cities were urban monsters draining life from the countryside; Paris was a place of excitement and the scene of events which might change the world.

Some ten years later Mercier sat down to write his *Le Nouveau Paris* (1798), a kind of progress report on how Paris had fared during the Revolution. His conclusions were, on the whole, rather gloomy, influenced by his own experiences during those turbulent years; although an avowed republican (elected to the National Convention in September 1792), he protested against the tyranny of the Terror and Jacobin rule, and was imprisoned for his pains.[9] He felt betrayed by the Revolution which he believed to have produced only criminal mediocrities perverting republican ideals into anarchy; a further experience of government, as a member of the Council of Five Hundred, from 1795–7, only added to his cynicism. Although *Le Nouveau Paris* is full of information on the manners and costume of the rabid Jacobins (whom he detested), and on the exaggerated styles worn by the leaders of fashion known to history as the *Incroyables* and the *Merveilleuses* in the raffish society of the Directory, Mercier's bitterness provides a barrier to objectivity; his more vitriolic comments have to be taken in conjunction with other contemporary accounts.

A revolution such as that of 1789, with its far-reaching effects on politics and society, was bound to polarize opinions; some people had never welcomed the Revolution, some felt (like Mercier) that its principles had been betrayed, and others felt they had not been achieved. Reading memoirs and eye-witness accounts of the period should be an exercise in caution; some of these works were written with obvious prejudices, some under political pressures (whether Jacobin, Thermidorean or post-Restauration) and some with the convenient amnesia of time. Foreign accounts are also notable for confirmed prejudices, and in any case, in a period of xenophobia created by violent social and political upheavals at home, and war on all fronts, the French were not disposed to encourage visitors from hostile countries − by the mid 1790s this meant much of Europe. At this time, as has been noted, there were no fashion magazines, and it was politically tactless even to talk about fashion; records (documentary, or in the form of actual garments) of the dress worn by the rich, or even the reasonably well-off, are rare even after the Terror, until things were on a calmer footing.

There is also, during the Revolution, a disparity in the kind of artistic sources available. In the early years, large-scale works immortalizing the heroic events of the Revolution were commissioned, but often unfinished as they were overtaken by fast-changing events;[10] topical prints of course exist (although many more were destroyed since their possession might be politically dangerous), but their bias and crudity can sometimes render them of limited use. A number of portrait artists were identified with the royalist cause and fled, along with their *émigré* clients, in the early days of the Revolution; others fled after 1792 or never returned from abroad where they had been studying. David, the greatest artist of the period, produced a number of fine portraits, but from 1792 his energies were increasingly channelled into politics and revolutionary festivals. During the Terror, the very concept of portraiture seemed bourgeois if not downright aristocratic; the business of existing was enough to occupy most people. Not until the later 1790s, under the Directory, was there a revival of portraiture, when the reality of life after the horrors of Robespierre's rule could be confirmed by the long-term commitment to posterity of images on canvas.

Not only was the Revolution a shock to the accepted wisdom of the eighteenth century that Reason should prevail in the works of Man, but it also showed how powerfully circumstances − even what might appear to be trivial events − could sway the destiny of a nation, and even of a continent. Over the period of some twenty years which this book covers, the events leading up to the Revolution, and triggered off by it, were of immense significance, both at the time and to the course of world history since. It would, in a book of this length, and with the main subject of dress, be inappropriate to discuss in detail the political and international ramifications of the Revolution (the reader will find a very brief outline of the main political events given in the Chronological Table). It should be stressed, however, that at no other time in history have politics and dress been so closely entwined as during the French Revolution; some examination of complex political ideas and events is unavoidable if this link is to be maintained.

It is sometimes easy to see the French Revolution as inevitable, the culmination of a process of intellectual ferment, a dying feudal regime racked with inequalities, and a weak king. Napoleon said, with the virtue of hindsight, that 'when a king is said to be a kind man, the reign is a failure'. Undoubtedly, Louis XVI, who succeeded to the throne in 1774, was a kind and well-meaning man; it is equally true that he was badly advised and not a natural ruler, and that he was content to let his ministers run the ship of state. There was no legislative body to restrict the royal will, and the only possible check on the king were the *Parlements* (higher courts) in which royal edicts had to be registered before they became law. The only national assembly was the Estates General, and that had not met since 1614.

23

Yet, of course, no thoughts of revolutionary upheaval troubled the *ancien régime* in the early 1780s. Although the late eighteenth century generally was a period of declining absolutism, due mainly to the slack hands and indifference of Louis XV, the monarchy was still the apex of the social pyramid, presiding over cleric, noble and commoner.

Out of a population of roughly 25 million, the First Estate, the clergy, comprised about 130,000. About half of these were 'regular' clergy (in abbeys and convents) and the rest were 'secular' clergy in charge of parishes; their income was derived from land and tithes, and like the nobility, they were exempt from most taxation. The Second Estate, the nobility, were about 200,000 in number. Within this group came the 'old' nobility, the *noblesse d'epée*, the original feudal aristocracy with attendant privileges such as the rights of local justice and rights to feudal dues, and the *noblesse de robe*, who held the main administrative, judicial and financial offices in the kingdom, and who dominated the *Parlements* and provincial local government. The rest of the population was the Third Estate, which ranged from the upper bourgeoisie of the cities, to the peasants (mostly tenants or hired labourers) in the countryside. Though there were vast regional variations, the Third Estate was subject to the heaviest taxation, and in a few areas there was still a state of serfdom, although this had been abolished on Crown lands in 1779.

Money – in the form of taxation and who paid it – was the besetting problem for the monarchy; France's financial troubles, exacerbated by foreign wars and her involvement in the American War of Independence, grew more acute as bankruptcy appeared to be inevitable. The later 1780s were dominated by the frustrated attempts of some of the more far-sighted royal ministers, such as the Swiss banker, Jacques Necker, to put financial reforms into effect; when attempts to tax the aristocracy and gentry were scuppered by the *Parlements*, it was decided in the summer of 1788 to summon the Estates General, as a last resort, to meet in May 1789.

It is the view of the historian Norman Hampson that the bankruptcy of the monarchy was 'the catalyst that fused the social tensions of France in a tremendous explosion'.[11] Yet throughout the 1780s, voices for reform had been gathering momentum, and the most obvious candidate for treatment was the nobility; it was, according to Alexis de Tocqueville's great classic, *The Ancien Régime and the French Revolution* (1856), the sight of unjust privileges and the 'ridiculous, ramshackle' institutions of France which encouraged thinking men towards reform. Such men, even at the highest levels of society, would be familiar with the doctrines of reason and humanity preached by the *philosophes* (and synthesized in Diderot's *Encyclopédie*) which helped to make the nation conscious of the fact that it was still governed by superstition and the barbarous relics of a feudal past. The basic equality of all men, setting aside accidents of birth, is best expressed in Figaro's famous address to Count Almaviva:

Parce que vous êtes un grand Seigneur, vous vous croyez un grand génie . . . noblesse, fortune, un rang, des places; tout cela rend si fier! qu'avez-voux fait pour tant de biens? vous vous êtes donné la peine de naître, & rien de plus; du reste homme assez ordinaire! tandis que moi . . .[12]

in a play that was, ironically enough, performed at court in 1784. It was de Tocqueville's thesis that, because the nobility were often remote from public affairs, they dabbled with the ideas of the *philosophes* as entertaining *jeux d'esprit*, matter for metaphysical argument and no more. Democracy, whatever it might mean, had been in fashion in France since the American War of Independence, and the Anglomania of the 1780s encouraged French visitors to travel to England[13] to see for themselves how the British political system (lauded, for example, by Voltaire and Montesquieu) actually worked.

Of all the *philosophes*, the most important (as inspiration behind the French Revolution) was Rousseau (1712–78); vague and visionary, his political philosophy could be interpreted in as many ways as there were to be different strands within the republican movement. He argued that since the ideal state is based on the virtue of its members, men should bind themselves together in a 'social contract' to be maintained through the operation of the 'Popular Will'; this is not necessarily the will of the majority, but of the best informed, but it must be based on the conscious assent of the governed. Rousseau's great contribution was to be the first to expound the basic principles of popular sovereignty; in an aristocratic society, he set out the virtues of the common man, and promoted the perfect political animal, the citizen.[14]

Themes like the 'citizen' and the 'rights of man' feature prominently in the journals and newspapers of the 1780s, as part of a heightened political awareness.[15] It has been estimated that more than two-thirds of men and a third of women in Paris on the eve of the Revolution were literate; journals were read aloud in public places, and even those who could not read could pick up the language and content of political discussion. It is not clear how far such ideas were current in the countryside; to begin with, at least, political discussion and revolutionary acts were an urban phenomenon.

Of all the classes in France, the middle class (small though it was compared to its equivalent in England) provided the firmest support for the new political ideas; with their ambitions frustrated by government and nobility, its members had most to gain from a change in the system, and it is not surprising to find that from 1789 the course of the Revolution was in their hands. Women, too, were not excluded from interest in political ideas. Admittedly many aristocrats had the surface enthusiasm of their class for anything modish, even for politics, but a number of intellectual women genuinely wished to be aware

of current trends; the works of the *philosophes* were discussed in the salons[16] of Madame Necker and the comtesse de Genlis, and Madame Roland (a future leading light of the Girondins) tells us that she was brought up to revere Rousseau.

Rousseau, however, claimed that women were by nature frivolous beings, whose natural role in life was to be wife and mother; it was through their virtue rather than their knowledge that society was to be regenerated. None of the *philosophes*, except Condorcet[17] during the Revolution, urged that women should have educational and political rights equal to those held by men; Rousseau's view on the inferiority of women was one which temperamentally suited the republican government.

The educational lot of women in France (as in Europe generally) was poor; there were *bibliothèques des dames*, digests of grammar, literature, history and travel, and there was some educational content in the fashion magazines of the decade, but much of this was inconsequential. Although not as anti-feminist as his hero Rousseau, Mercier also felt that women's progress was hindered by their love of fashion and vanity; their education, such as it was – 'leçons de coquetterie et de vanité' – taught them only to want a life of pleasure and extravagance.[18] At the same time (and Mercier seems blithely unconcerned at the many contradictions in his work), the fashion industry, of which France is the undoubted leader, is found essential to the French economy.

Fashion was not just a fundamental part of French industry, but a way of life, particularly for upper-class women with very little to do except to enjoy a life of pleasure. Not all aristocratic women were like the marquise de Merteuil, in Laclos's *Les Liaisons Dangereuses* (1782), with her cynicism and profligacy, but a life of indolence could easily lead to undue emphasis on the charms of intrigue and the pleasures of fashion. Such women would spend hours at their toilettes, and in choosing their costumes for the various

activities of the day – the music lessons, the rides in the Bois de Boulogne, the walks in the Tuileries Gardens, the rounds of visits, the intimate suppers and the evening entertainments (operas, balls, soirées etc.), which formed the bounds of their existence.

At the apex of the social structure was the court, which, since the days of Louis XIV, provided the leadership of fashion and taste. Even Mercier, with his republican sympathies, admits in the *Tableau de Paris* that 'La Cour est le centre de la politesse, parce qu'elle y donne le ton des usages & des manières', and Madame de Genlis, in spite of her flirtation with revolutionary ideas through her intimacy with the Orléanist faction, acknowledged in her old age that the French court was the model for all the courts of Europe.

The *grand habit de cour*, which consisted of a heavily boned bodice, layered lace sleeves, a heavily trimmed skirt worn over a vast hoop, and a long train which it needed considerable practice to manage, was the most formal costume worn at court. It had to be worn for 'les grandes cérémonies d'étiquette', such as court presentations, solemn religious occasions, and formal court balls. Although the queen, Marie-Antoinette, reduced the number of occasions on which full court dress had to be worn, it was seen to be, in its outdated style and expensive, over-trimmed

---

2 *Self-portrait with two pupils, Mlle Marie-Gabrielle Capet, and Mlle Carreaux de Rosemond*, 1785, Adélaïde Labille-Guiard.

Seated at her easel – the work has been seen as a propaganda piece urging that women should have a greater say in the *Académie* – the artist in her satin *robe à l'anglaise* is fashionably if impractically dressed for painting. The pupil who gazes at the canvas (probably Marie-Gabrielle Capet) is also dressed in a *robe à l'anglaise*, a subdued olive-green silk, with a lawn kerchief, sleeve ruffles and cap.

luxury, increasingly absurd, emphasizing the gap between the court and ordinary fashion.

Unlike the timid Louis XVI who was content to wear what was put before him, Marie-Antoinette had decided tastes in fashion. The arrangement of her wardrobe has been well documented; officially, 'douze grands habits de cour, douze petites robes dites de fantaisie, douze robes riches sur panier pour le jeu ou le souper des petits appartements' were ordered for her three times a year,[19] and many, more informal, outfits were provided for her as necessary.

Other than court dress with its rich silks and sumptuous decoration, the formal *robe de cérémonie à la française* was the sacque dress, worn over a hoop and also heavily trimmed; in the 1780s this was accepted at court except on very formal occasions, and at Fontainebleau and Marly where it was not the custom to wear the *grand habit*. Slightly less formal was the *robe parée*, which we might call evening dress, and which, at court, was worn for evening entertainments and for dining in the *petits appartements* at Versailles; this gown could take the form of a sacque or a *robe à l'anglaise*, but it had to be elegantly trimmed and worn over a hoop. *Robes de fantaisie* were less formal robes, such as *polonaises* or simpler *robes à l'anglaise*, and worn without a hoop. If this seems confusing to the reader, it could be equally so to a lady unused to court attendance; the court was a pitfall for the unwary, where everything was regulated by custom and etiquette and where the less than elegant choice and management of dress and accessories was eagerly noted by the censorious.

With the growing penetration of English influence in the 1780s, the tight-bodied *robe à l'anglaise* was all the rage; the fitted bodice curved down at the centre front and centre back, and the gown was either cut in one with the bodice leading into the skirt, or with a complete division at the waist, the skirt being set with tiny pleats into the bodice. As this was an open robe (the usual style for most dresses in the eighteenth

3 *Fashion plate*, 1787, from the *Gallerie des Modes et Costumes.*

This back view of the *robe à l'anglaise* shows the later style of this dress with the bodice cut separately from the skirt; the fashionable width at the sides and the back of the gown is created by hip pads attached to the stays beneath. In a decade dominated by Anglomania in dress, the hat, too, with its foliage-like feathers, lattice ribbons and lace brim, is described as a 'chapeau à l'Anglomane'.

Gallerie des Modes in 1778. The fashion magazines also refer to the *robe à la circassienne*, a version of the looped-up *polonaise* with short sleeves and other 'oriental' trimmings such as fur and tassels; there was also a *robe à la Turque* which could have similar exotic decorations, but which was mainly distinguished by a long train falling on the ground. Whatever the minor differences in ornamentation and arrangement of overskirt, the basic dress of the 1780s was the tight-bodied robe, which did not alter radically in style

4 *Fashion plate*, 1786, from the *Cabinet des Modes.*

This *robe à la turque* with its elaborate decoration is clearly a gown for a grand occasion. The *robe* is of embroidered red satin, and the skirt is of white silk embroidered with flowers and trimmed with ribbon.

century), it was worn with a skirt, usually of different material to the robe. The desired effect was for a tiny waist, with the skirt flaring out at the sides and back; this could be achieved by small pads or bustles, or by lifting up the overskirt and arranging it in three swags of material, a style known as a *polonaise* and first noted in the

5 *Marie Charlotte Louise Perrette Aglaé, comtesse de la Châtre*, 1789, Elisabeth Louise Vigée Le Brun.

Although the sitter's husband, *Premier Gentilhomme* to Louis XVI's younger brother the comte de Provence, left France soon after the fall of the Bastille and later joined the army of the princes at Koblenz, the sitter's opinions were more liberal, and along with other aristocratic ladies she helped to prepare the Champ de Mars for the *Fête de la Fédération* on 14 July 1790. She eventually left for England when the Jacobins came to power. Her costume is a casually elegant white dotted muslin open robe and skirt, a linen *fichu* crossed over her breast; round her waist is a satin ribbon which matches the decoration in her wide-brimmed hat.

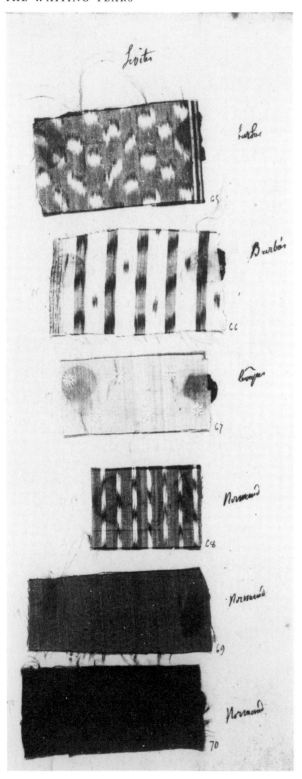

6 *Two pages from Marie-Antoinette's dress book for 1782.*

The Archives Nationales contains a book of dress samples for 1782 (78 have survived), from which the queen would choose those costumes which were needed for the various functions of the day. Beside the small swatches of material are listed the silk merchants from which the fabrics had been bought, Barbier and Lenormand being two of the most fashionable firms in Paris. Both for the *lévites* (a popular informal style, usually in the form of a wrapping gown tied around the waist with a sash), and the *robes sur le petit panier* (formal dresses worn over hoops), tiny design motifs are popular, small stylized flower patterns, stripes, dots etc. *Chiné* silks were particularly fashionable for *lévites*, as can be seen from numbers 65, 66 and 68.

throughout the period. The decoration of the gown, therefore, assumed a great importance, and this was the province of the *marchande(e) des modes*:

Son art n'est pas de fabriquer aucune chose; il consiste à former ingénieusement des résultats nouveaux, des ornemens variés & gracieux de toutes les productions légères des autres arts & particulièrement de celles du passementier.[20]

Passementerie encompassed all kinds of braid, lace, ribbons and other trimmings, and the adroit modiste would arrange them according to the law of perfect taste and the 'caprice du moment'. The greatest modiste of all, Rose Bertin, was particularly adept at incorporating the 'caprice du moment' into her *ensembles*; she was highly successful at the elaborate head-dresses known as *poufs*, and during the early 1780s her creations celebrated, for example, Franco-American victories in the American War of Independence, and Montgolfier ascending in his balloon.

The marquis de Valfons in 1786 noted that there were 250 ways of trimming a dress; these included ribbons with names like 'désespoir', 'oeil abbatu', 'attentions marquées' and so on.[21] That summer the *Cabinet des Modes* noted that at Morlière's ribbon shop in the rue St Honoré, there were 'Rubans à la Cagliostro' of pink edged with green and decorated with pyramids (Cagliostro was an Italian adventurer who travelled in Europe and the Near East, dabbling in the occult); another popular design on sale was a 'Ruban au Diadème Arc-en-Ciel', striped with rose, green, white and violet and zig-zagged in white. Such ribbons would look their best on the plain silks which were in fashion for everyday dress in the 1780s. The *Cabinet des Modes* (1 June 1786) declared that ladies of fashion would wear nothing but taffeta; light, thin silks such as *taffetas de Florence* and *taffetas d'Angleterre* (both made in France) were all the rage. In commissions to Jean Nicholas Barbier, silk merchant to the Queen and to ladies of fashion, plain taffetas proved to

be the most popular silks for all kinds of garments – dresses, *redingotes*, jackets, skirts, mantles; they are closely followed by gowns of white gauze or muslin worn over white taffeta skirts.[22]

Fifteen thousand looms were in operation in Lyons on the eve of the Revolution, producing the large-patterned woven silks demanded by court/formal dress, and the lighter silks with tiny motifs – stylized flowers, dots and dashes or

7 *Brocaded silk (detail of dress), c. 1782–3.*

Textile designs, like costume itself, could echo current affairs and fashionable fads. Here the designer has incorporated, between the small bunches of flowers, tiny balloons, reflecting the craze of the early 1780s – the first unmanned balloon ascent took place in 1782, and in the following year the Montgolfier brothers made a successful trip in a fire balloon.

8 *Queen Marie-Antoinette, c.* 1783, after Elisabeth
Louise Vigée Le Brun.

The artist most associated with portraits of the French
queen, Vigée Le Brun succeeds in transforming the
rather plain royal features – the aquiline nose and the
thick Habsburg lower lip – into the image of a
fashionable regal beauty. Moving away from the
formality of official court portraiture, Marie-Antoinette is depicted in the fake pastoral simplicity of the
Petit Trianon, with her deceptively simple (but expensive) muslin chemise tied around the waist with a
gold-striped sash, and a wide-brimmed straw hat
decorated with silk ribbons and a panache of ostrich
plumes.

impressionistic *chiné*[23] designs – which high fashion required. With constantly changing fashions, a trend encouraged by the fashion magazines, silk designers and merchants had to keep abreast of current tastes; a growth in consumerism encouraged women to covet more in the way of dress, and since plain silks were cheaper to produce than more complicated woven ones, the manufacturers of Lyons provided the former in large quantities. They were also uneasily aware of the possible threat posed to their business by the popularity of foreign-made fabrics catering to the new vogue for simplicity, such as English gauzes and cottons, and fine muslin from India exported by the British East India Company; the *Eden-Vergennes Treaty* (1786) secured favourable conditions for the export of such materials to France.

The finest muslin, as soft and as white as snowflakes, according to one poetic commentator, came from India; worn with transparent English gauze, such a costume could be seen on the queen herself when she relaxed, with her coterie, at the Petit Trianon. 'Malgré l'hiver, beaucoup de femmes se mettent encore en blanc; c' est-à-dire en robe de mousseline,' stated the *Cabinet des Modes* in November 1785. Such muslin could be made into robes (open gowns) or into the all-in-one chemise gown popularized by Marie-Antoinette when pregnant in 1778 with her first child. This *chemise à la reine* was very popular in the 1780s.[24] It was, of course, the dress which caused a scandal when the queen was depicted in it, in a portrait by Vigée Le Brun which was exhibited at the Salon in 1783. The impropriety of painting a formal portrait of the queen in this simple gown with its connotations of *déshabillé*, never seems to have occurred to the artist. Vigée Le Brun herself had, during the 1780s, helped to set the fashion for such modes by wearing a similar costume herself, even when painting the queen (except at Versailles where full dress had to be worn), and by persuading her

9 *Fashion plate*, 1786, from the *Cabinet des Modes*.

This ensemble consists of a white foulard chemise spotted in yellow and trimmed with black, and a hat in martial style, a *casque à la Bellona*.

aristocratic sitters to be depicted in quasi-classical mode and with unpowdered hair.

Powdered hair and an artificial complexion were *de rigueur* for formal occasions,[25] but by the end of the 1780s a number of women found such an appearance inappropriate, when they wore the simpler styles of dress which Anglomania had brought into vogue. These included English riding habits which consisted of a matching jacket and skirt, with contrasting waistcoat; other popular jackets (often made of linen or cotton) were the *caraco* and the *pierrot*, tight-fitting bodices with flirtatious short basques, diminished occasionally to just a back frill.

Another garment inspired by Anglomania was the *redingote*, an open robe based on the Englishman's riding coat; it is first mentioned in the *Gallerie des Modes* in 1786, and early the following year it is described as a 'robe Franco-Anglomane' in the *Magasin des Modes*. Tight to the body, like a *robe à l'anglaise*, and with similar long close-fitting sleeves, it usually incorporated masculine features such as a caped collar and a waistcoat; it was versatile enough to be worn outdoors or indoors depending on the fabrics used, and could be worn with a matching or contrasting skirt. Another coat-like garment was the *douillette*, which was looser-fitting and covered the whole garment beneath, often tying at the front with ribbon bows. The actress Louise Fusil remembered that the fashionable *demi-toilettes* just before the Revolution were *redingotes*, and *douillettes* of satin.[26]

All commentators who remarked on fashions in France noted the enormous variety in styles for women, from the complexities of formal dress, to the simplicities of undress. Some, like Mercier, while claiming to deplore the extravagance involved, found such variety in adornment to be a sign of the French genius for elegance in display. Others, like Rigoley de Juvigny, found no redeeming element in the feminine love of finery; the extremes in dress to which women

10 *Honorée-Suzanne Marceau Desgraviers*, 1784, Antoine-François Sergent-Marceau.

This quiet domestic scene depicts the sitter fashionably but simply dressed in a *caraco* jacket and matching skirt.

11 *Fashion plate*, 1787, from the *Magasin des Modes Nouvelles*.

Overshadowing this *demi-redingote* of striped taffeta is a vast hat, trimmed with ribbon and crowned with ostrich plumes.

enduring strain of anti-clericalism) appear not just in the deadly affectations of *Les Liaisons Dangereuses*, but in the world of thinking men and women of the upper and middle classes. This was often allied (and such feelings were not seen as mutually contradictory) to the new pre-Romantic cult of 'sensibility' – that is, an exceptional openness to emotional impressions, to the force of passion and a heightened sense of identity with 'nature'; the leader of this movement was Rousseau who in his writings (his *Confessions*, his *Émile*, his *Nouvelle Héloïse*), made the examination of mental sensations into a work of art. Rousseau was at one with the other *philsophes* (a state of affairs that was the exception rather than the rule) in his criticism of the way that society was organized; he placed particular emphasis on the corruptive nature of the aristocracy. The assertion of a new middle-class morality which challenged aristocratic traditions (the worst of these were hypocrisy, insensibility and amorality) first manifested itself in England; it was marked by an independence of outlook both in politics and in art[28] and contained both a new realism and a new emphasis on homely virtues like self-reliance and pride in work. Voltaire admired such attitudes when he came to London in the 1720s and in his *Letters concerning the English Nation* urged them on his fellow-countrymen.

The admiration expressed by such writers for the sturdy practicalities of English life, coupled with a growing unease regarding the role played by the aristocracy in France, contributed much to the Anglomania of the 1780s. Although on occasions of grandeur men wore formal full dress – the silk coat (*habit*) and knee-breeches (*culottes*)

were prone were, he opined, due to 'l'esprit du siècle, à l'égoisme universel né du philosophisme'.[27]

The works of the *philosophes*, inspired by reason, truth and tolerance, had to some extent led to an undermining of society; a mood of cynicism and attacks on morality (including an

12 *Portrait of a young woman in a broad-brimmed hat*, 1783, Henri Pierre Danloux.

The large frizzed and curled *coiffure* is outlined by the jaunty angle at which the ribboned hat is placed. The sitter is dressed for outdoors in her *redingote* and pleated muslin *jabot*.

trimmed with gold or silver braid, and the elegant embroidered *veste* or formal, skirted waistcoat – this costume was seen to be in decline. This may partly be due to the indifference of the monarch to fine clothes, but more to a general reduction in splendour at court. The *Cabinet des Modes* (15 May 1786) noted that it was becoming increasingly rare to see women in 'robes de Grande Parure' or gentlemen in 'Habits à la Françoise, avec le chapeau sous le bras, & l'épée au côté'.[29] Mercier addressed himself to the man of fashion: '... mets des dentelles; que ta veste soit brodée; galonne ton habit; fais-toi coëffer à l'oiseau royal; porte un petit chapeau sous le bras ...'.[30] But this was mere rhetoric, for all this – the elegant, superbly decorated silk suit, the hair formally pomaded and powdered (the wig or coiffure *à l'oiseau royal* was a style with brushed-out wings at the side, popular in the 1760s and 1770s) and the hat carried under the arm so as not to disturb the hair – was, as Mercier was aware, increasingly far removed from the world of fashion.

13 *La marquise de Fresne d'Aguesseau*, 1789, Elisabeth Louise Vigée Le Brun

This is a particularly stylish ensemble which helps to explain why the artist was so popular with her fashionable society sitters. The marquise wears a dark red velvet robe (probably a *redingote*) over a chemise of fine muslin; this dress has a drawstring neck edged with gold, and the skirt (worn over a silk underskirt) is patterned in gold spots. Complementing this chemise is a turban of white and gold silk gauze. The marquise's earrings are gold hoops with mother-of-pearl pendants, and fixed to her belt is a Wedgwood cameo, identified as 'Poor Maria' seated under a weeping willow with her faithful dog, a subject taken from Laurence Sterne's popular pre-Romantic novel, *A Sentimental Journey* (1768).

The reduction of splendour at court ceremonies, partly due to the taste of the times, and also to the need for royal economies, helped to produce a more casual attitude towards the monarchy. One of Louis XVI's pages, Félix d'Hézecques, writing after the Revolution, remarks: 'Je suis bien loin de penser que le retranchement d'un costume, d'une cérémonie pompeuse, puisse faire une révolution,' but it had to be acknowledged that any discussion about 'les causes de notre bouleversement général' had to include some mention of the contribution made by indifference in dress at the highest level.[31]

Caraccioli (writing under the guise of 'an Indian at Paris'), noted that one of the 'Follies and Extravagancies of the Times' was the propensity of the man of fashion, even in company, to wear 'the most slovenly dress, for which he makes no apology, but a bow or a caper, declaring that he is a warm admirer of English customs'.[32] On the same lines we find the comte de Ségur commenting: 'The laws of England were studied and envied by men of a mature age; English horses and jockeys, boots and coats after the English fashion, could alone suit the fancy of young men'. It was his view that such styles had helped to undermine authority.[33]

The main aristocratic promoter of Anglomania was Philippe, duc d'Orléans, leader of fashion, and of a powerful anti-court faction. He was a crony of the Prince of Wales, and instrumental in popularizing English aristocratic pastimes like high gambling, and horse-racing in the 1780s. From England also in this decade came the institution of the club, which was, during the Revolution, to assume a political complexion. Orléans's championship of revolutionary views was well known (during the Revolution he became Philippe-Egalité) and a constant source of irritation to the monarchy; no doubt it was also to emphasize his distance from the court that he and his followers so enthusiastically adopted English fashions which proclaimed their sympathy with the new ideas.

Pl. 160

Le Clere del.

Dupin Sculp.

Duc et Paire décoré des Ordres du Roi occupant une des premieres places à la Cour. Il est vetu d'un hábit d'été brodé.

14 *Fashion plate*, 1781, from the *Gallerie des Modes et Costumes*.

This ducal fashion figure is the epitome of aristocratic grandeur in his embroidered *habit à la française*. At court, formal dress also demanded the powdered wig, the *chapeau bras*, and the display of knightly orders. Here we see the cross with the dove of the Saint-Esprit, and its blue ribbon ('un large ruban bleu céleste moiré') worn across the waistcoat, and the smaller cross of the military order of St Louis suspended by a red ribbon from the buttonhole.

15 *Fashion plate*, 1786, from the *Cabinet des Modes*.

This stylish young *élégant* wears a cloth frock coat with velvet collar; the buttons, says the editor, are the size of 'un écu de trois livres'. His *gilet* is of pink satin, his breeches of yellow cotton; on his head is a hat *à l'Androsmane*, and he carries a bamboo cane.

What were these fashions which so enraged the conservative/Francophile in taste? The most obvious item was the caped English greatcoat, which Mercier describes as 'les redingotes de Londres avec leurs triples collets & leur camail'; such a coat was long, straight, and ungainly – in Mercier's eyes – when compared with the formal, cut-away elegance of the French coat.[34] Another English fashion, the frock coat with its easy fit, fairly unstructured lines and small collar, had for some years been popular in France; with this *fraque*, could be worn the *veston* (a waistcoat, sometimes with sleeves, and with short, rounded skirts) or the *gilet* (a sleeveless waistcoat with no skirts, cut straight across at the front and often, by the late 1780s, double-breasted).

With the greatcoat or frock, men wore starched, puffed-out cravats, thick stockings, and their own hair – 'les cheveux ronds, plats & sans poudre' (Mercier). Another sight inimical to the traditional French perception of elegance, was that men wore their hats on their heads instead of under their arms. Such hats could be either the popular jockey caps (Mercier tells us that the equestrian theme was further borne out by the way in which French *élégants* carried a riding whip) or large, round hats which one writer describes as being worn almost covering the nose so that their wearers looked like Quakers.[35]

It is not always easy to judge how widely certain fashions were adopted; the prejudices of the moralists sometimes overwhelm their objective judgement. No doubt the young men addicted to fashion as a way of life (whom Mercier usually calls, in the phrase of the *ancien régime*, the

16 *Fashion plate, c. 1789.*

This rather etiolated figure – typical of the languid young men promoted in the pages of the fashion magazines – achieves an admired slimness of silhouette by his very long tight-fitting *surtout* and his fondness for stripes. Although sometimes derided as an effeminate fashion for men, the large fur muff was a fashionable accessory in the 1780s.

petits maîtres, but whom we will call, anticipating the fashion journals of the Revolution and post-revolutionary period, the *élégants*), wore extreme versions of English dress when it was the vogue to do so; in the same way they defied convention in the 1790s by adopting some elements of arisotcratic costume against the prevailing republican aesthetic. Yet it does seem that the ease and

17 Illustration from *Costumes des Moeurs et de l'Esprit François avant la Grande Révolution*, 1791, Louis Binet.

One of a series of illustrations to Mercier's *Tableau de Paris*, this plate points out the difference in dress and deportment between the French and the English styles. Quoting from Mercier, the anonymous compiler of the *Costumes des Moeurs* notes: 'C'est le ton aujourdhui de copier l'Anglois dans son habillement. On a l'habit long, étroit, le chapeau sur la tête, la cravate bouffante, les gants, les cheveux courts & la badine.'

Echoing Mercier's preference for the elegancies of French costume with its powdered wig, formal suit, sword and *chapeau bras*, the rhetorical question is posed: 'N'avons-nous autres choses à imiter des Anglois que la forme de leur habillement?'

18 *Antoine-Laurent Lavoisier and his wife Marie-Anne-Pierrette*, 1788, Jacques–Louis David.

The pioneering chemist (possibly working here on his *Traité élémentaire de chimie*, published in 1789) wears the sober black suit of the professional man. His wife wears her hair in the mass of frizzed curls and long unravelling ringlets popular from the mid 1780s. Her dress is of fine white muslin over a silk underskirt, and the collar is of embroidered muslin; a long tasselled sash is worn round her waist.

simplicity of English modes were admired and copied at all levels of society where there was a perception of the meaning of fashion.

As well as the sporting look on which most of the fashion magazines concentrate, the English taste also inclined towards a dark, sober costume; this was the black suit, worn by middle-class businessmen and the professional man – the lawyer, the doctor, the official – which was to become urban dress of nineteenth-century man. Arthur Young, in Paris in 1787, noted that men 'of small or moderate fortune' wore black suits and stockings; this, admittedly, was partly on account of the mud and the dirt in the streets of the capital, exacerbated by the custom for young men of fashion to dash around in one-horse cabriolets. Mercier adds that frequent court mourning was in tune with the taste for black,

'car l'habit noir s'accorde merveilleusement avec les boues, l'intempérance des saisons, l'économie, & la répugnance à faire une longue toilette'.[36]

The conflict, if we can see it in that way, between French dress with its traditional concentration on luxury and uniformity, and the English intake of greater individualism and freedom in attire, seemed to have been resolved, by the end of the 1780s, in favour of the latter. The last word will be Arthur Young's comment in 1789:

When they had nothing better to attend to, the fashionable Parisians were correctness itself in all that pertained to the toilette, and were therefore thought a frivolous people; but now they have something of more importance than dress to occupy them, and the light airy character that was usually given them will have no foundation in truth.[37]

2 | Politics and Fashion 1789–1794

In a mood of desperation, Louis XVI was persuaded in 1788 to call the Estates General; this seemed the only way out of the impasse of the government's inability to make the privileged classes contribute to the running of the state. All France, which for some months had been agog with restlessness and rumour, began the process of electing representatives; by the end of April the following year some 1200 deputies had been elected. Grievances (*cahiers de doléances*) were drafted, which embodied both the vague rhetoric of the *philosophes* – the rights of man and the duties of society – and more concrete proposals such as tax reform, the abolition of feudal rights, fairly administered justice and the curtailment of clerical privileges. A rash of publications, some anonymous, some signed, testified to the suddenly released energy of a people straining for some political expression.

'The ferment at Paris is beyond conception' was the comment made by Arthur Young in the capital in the summer of 1789; people stopped him in the street to talk about politics, pamphlets offered a variety of viewpoints and the talk in the cafés was all about the latest developments in the many factions which had suddenly appeared, as if from underground. Young's sympathies were on the side of change, which he declared to be 'necessary for the happiness of the people' and he attacked the court party as 'supine' and 'stupid'. Yet on his travels outside Paris he found one gentleman who thought that civil war would be inevitable, and 'it is now only by torrents of blood that we have any hope of establishing a freer constitution'.[1] In the spirit of optimism which prevailed in 1789, this kind of prophetic warning would have been regarded as very much out of step, at least in official circles.

The opening session of the Estates General was to take place at Versailles on 5 May in the presence of the King. As the Estates General had not met since 1614, the Grand-Master of Ceremonies, the marquis de Brézé, sent out in April instructions regarding the costume which had to be worn by the deputies. The First Estate, the clergy, were to wear the ecclesiastical dress appropriate to their status within the Church, which could range from the scarlet silk of cardinals to the black stuff cassock of the humble parish priest. The Second Estate wore dress suitable to their aristocratic rank; this comprised a coat and *veste* of black silk or cloth (according to the season) trimmed with gold braid, and with a matching cloak, black silk breeches, white stockings, a lace cravat, a sword, and a hat with feathers *à la Henri IV*, 'comme celui des chevaliers de l'ordre' – that is, the order of the St Esprit, the most noble order of French chivalry, founded in 1578.

The Third Estate, consisting of half the deputies, were ordered to wear suits of black cloth, black stockings, and short cloaks of black silk like those worn by lawyers and the *noblesse de robe*; they had to wear a plain muslin cravat and a black three-cornered hat, and – as they were not recognized as gentlemen – they were not entitled to a sword.

To an English doctor, Edward Rigby, who saw the three Estates taking part in the formal procession entering Paris after the fall of the Bastille, the difference between the splendid costume worn by the 'noblesse' and the higher orders of the clergy, and that worn by the Third Estate, was striking; their dress was 'very ordinary, even worse than that of the inferior sort of gownsmen at the English universities'.[2] He

Quid sum?   Je suis Citoyen.   Je suis Député du Tiers.

19 *The Three Estates*, 1789.

In contrast to the affected gestures and rich clothing of the First and Second Estates, the *Député du Tiers* with his simple demeanour and sombre costume proclaims himself the proud representative of the people.

noted, however, that it was the Third Estate, however poorly attired, that received the applause of the crowds.

The sartorial apartheid caused great offence because it was held to be an affront to the dignity of those who represented the majority of the people of France. 'Une loi ridicule & bizarre nous est imposée en arrivant', was the comment made by an anonymous deputy of the Third Estate; such a decree, ordered by the 'grand-maître des puérilités de la cour' only helped to enforce the class distinctions which he had hoped would be avoided in this assembly in which the hopes of the nation rested. While admitting that dress in itself was a thing of little importance, when it symbolized the hopes and aspirations of a people, it *was* significant; dress should not be a barrier to unity and the assembly should not be degraded by etiquette and subject to a 'mascarade indécente'.[3]

There were a number of protests against these dress regulations, among the most vociferous being that of the comte de Mirabeau, a spokesman for the Third Estate, who declared that they felt affronted at not being allowed to wear plumes and lace had they so wished; what they wanted was to wear their own, everyday costume without dictatorship. The provincial deputy, whose opinions are quoted above, declared that he would wear his own clothes the better to preserve his character and his liberty.[4] It seems likely that most members of the Third Estate, except on ceremonial occasions, soon discarded the court-imposed rules, which became increasingly irrelevant as the pace of events quickened; they were abolished on 15 October 1789.

When it became clear that, under the system of voting by Estates, any notion of political progress would be blocked by the first two, the Third Estate, led by Mirabeau, withdrew from the proceedings, and finding themselves locked out from their customary meeting place, took refuge in what must be the most famous tennis court in

LISTE DE MM.ᵉˢ LES DEPUTÉS *de Paris*
a l'Assemblée Nationale

Dédiée l'Assemblée Nationale?

20 *Deputies from Paris to the National Assembly*, 1789

With Fame sounding her trumpet flying overhead, a triumphal chariot bears the deputies from Paris, dressed in sober black towards a National Assembly. They include among their number M Bailly, Dr Guillotin and the abbé Sieyès.

history, and declared that they would not part until 'the constitution of the kingdom was established on solid foundations'. This crucial act of defiance set the Third Estate in direct conflict with the King, who was eventually forced to agree to the idea of a 'National Assembly'; the more liberal section of the nobility and most of the clergy joined them.

It was the events of this heroic day in June, that David celebrates in his famous *Oath of the Jeu de Paume* of 1971 (see fig. 21). David was there himself, and saw men enthusiastically taking the oath by throwing their hats in the air, and catching them on the points of their canes.[5] As a work of propaganda (commissioned by the Jacobin Club) it is a mixture of truth and fiction. It combines spontaneous excitement with the carefully staged depiction of the heroes of the hour (such as the abbé Sieyès who helped to devise the constitutional framework for this and succeeding political systems, the president of the Assembly Jean-Sylvain Bailly, and the comte de Mirabeau), and future leaders such as Robespierre, who was not at all conspicuous on this occasion, but is here tactfully placed in a prominent position. Looking

21 *Le Serment du Jeu de Paume*, 1791, Jacques-Louis David.

In David's unfinished sketch (commissioned by the Assembly in 1791) the scene is the taking of the oath in the tennis court at Versailles. Jean-Sylvain Bailly, President of the National Assembly from 20 June 1789, stands on a table in the centre to declaim the oath; the abbé Sieyès sits to the right. In the group behind Sieyès, Robespierre clutches his breast, and Mirabeau strikes a dramatic pose in the right foreground. Laymen and clerics are symbolically united for the good of the country, and a bare-legged *sans-culotte* with ragged *bonnet rouge* observes the proceedings from the left. In the heroic gesture made familiar by David's famous *Oath of the Horatii* (1784), the main protagonists raise their arms to take the oath.

at this scene through the eyes of David (and noting the visual references to his great classical history paintings of the 1780s), it is clear that the artist wished to show free men in dress suited to 'republican' ideals. Since most of the deputies of the Third Estate were middle-class (the complicated franchise system favoured the urban and professional bourgeoisie), their favoured costume was the type of plain, cloth English-style suits and greatcoats which David depicts in his epic, unfinished work, an heroic commemoration of the events of 20 June 1789.

Confusion, fear and rumour invaded Paris in the summer of that year. The court party tried to spur the king into firm action, the nobility was worried about its centuries-old privileges being whittled away, and the new National Assembly feared an aristocratic backlash – the arrival of the Flanders regiment at Versailles and accounts of how it had trampled the tricolour under foot at a

REVEIL DU TIERS ETAT.

Ma feinte, il etoit tems que je me réveillasse, car l'oppression de mes fers me donnoient le cochemar un peu trop fort.

22 'Réveil du Tiers Etat', 1789.

While the Bastille is demolished in the background, the Third Estate (in the person of a respectably dressed member of the middle class) begins to break his chains, while the abbé (the First Estate) and the army officer (the Second Estate) look on with horror.

court banquet early in October inflamed public opinion, and caused Parisians to be apprehensive of a possible aristocratic reaction. The situation of the poor, whose concern for the provision of cheap and plentiful food was the main motivation for revolutionary activity, was particularly acute because of the disastrous harvest of 1788.

Although Paris was slowly being improved, and paved on the London model (according to Mercier, one-third of Paris had been rebuilt since the late 1780s), it was still basically a medieval city, with a working-class population alarmingly increased by a series of industrial and agricultural crises and pushed into cramped and appalling conditions. In such a situation, and with the power of rumour to breed fear, riots were easy to provoke, the most famous being the storming of the Bastille on 14 July. The immediate cause of this event was the dismissal by the king of Necker on 11 July; linked in the public mind with reforming policies (however ineffectual they had

23 *Une fête au Colisée*, François-Louis-Joseph Watteau, known as Watteau de Lille II.

A visible sign of the Anglomania of the late eighteenth century, the Colisée in the suburbs of Lille at Canteleu was built in 1786 in imitation of the London pleasure gardens at Vauxhall. Among the well-dressed crowds strolling in the grounds and dining in the pavilion, can be seen some fashionable enthusiasts for the Revolution as witnessed by their adoption of the tricolour cockade; even the children are adorned in this way. The preponderance of 'lampshade' hats and the style of the costume generally indicates the late summer of 1789.

been) Necker was seen as a hero and his departure from office was the catalyst which set Paris alight. Marie Grosholtz, later Madame Tussaud, in her memoirs remembered the mob rushing to her uncle's waxworks museum on the boulevard du Temple and seizing busts of Necker, and the duc d'Orléans (another popular anti-court figure) to carry about the streets.

The fall of the Bastille had more symbolic than practical importance, for very few prisoners were found in this royal fortress, and its attackers paid a heavy cost in the numbers of dead and wounded. It was seen, however, as the first significant blow against a traditional bastion of monarchical oppression. Its demolition seemed

also to signal the release of class hostility which had always been present throughout the eighteenth century, but which now, encouraged by the long-term publications of the *philosophes*, and the shorter-term impact of recent political events and economic troubles, became an important factor in society. The fall of the Bastille reverberated around France, inspiring rural revolts and the burning of châteaux as old scores were paid off; poor harvests and a feeling of unrest helped to encourage bands of the destitute who roamed the countryside and contributed much to the *grande peur* in the late summer months of 1789. Urged on by the unrest in the countryside, the National Assembly abolished feudal rights, and in early October brought back the king from Versailles to Paris to preside over the dismantling of the established order.

Having settled in the royal riding school (the manège) on the north side of the gardens of the Tuileries, the Assembly proceeded to pass a number of major reforms as laid down in the *Declaration of the Rights of Man*. This manifesto of the revolutionary bourgeoisie included the protection of property, freedom of conscience and the press, equality before the law, and equality of taxation and access to office.

Over the next few months, far-reaching reforms were set in motion. These included the reorganization of local administration in France (*départements* replaced the old provinces)[6], a new judicial system (elected judges and trial by jury) and the accountability of the clergy to the state.

Male suffrage was extended in a system considerably more democratic than that of England; deputies, however, were still men of substance and had to be elected by fairly prosperous 'active' citizens over 25 years of age.[7] Active citizens also had the right to join the National Guard, a militia initially set up by the electors of Paris to safeguard their property in what was seen as the collapse of the old order and established authority in the uneasy aftermath of the fall of the Bastille. The new *commune* of Paris chose Bailly as mayor

and the marquis de Lafayette (who had fought in the American War of Independence) as commander of the National Guard. Lafayette designed the tricolour which from the summer of 1789 became the most popular symbol of patriotism; red and blue were the colours of the city of Paris and white was the Bourbon colour. Red, white and blue were the colours of the uniforms of the National Guard, a prominent and popular sight in the streets of Paris, as they were seen to be a safeguard for the achievements of the Revolution. Imbued with revolutionary fervour, provincial militia along similar lines, the *fédérés*, were formed all over France, and they played a major part in the celebrations held in July 1790 to mark the anniversary of the fall of the Bastille; at the *Fête de la Fédération* held in the Champ de Mars (the present site of the Eiffel Tower) they were the visible symbol of the unity of the nation and its determination to carry through the goals of the Revolution.

Men and women of all classes had physically laboured to turn the Champ de Mars into a huge amphitheatre with tiers of seats. A flight of steps, formed from stones taken from the Bastille, led to an Altar of Liberty on which were placed the traditional symbols of royal authority such as the sceptre and the Hand of Justice with the addition of a spear bearing a Cap of Liberty. Talleyrand, the free-thinking bishop of doubtful morals (and, since February, President of the Assembly) celebrated mass in the presence of the King and Queen, the members of the Assembly, and a huge crowd of spectators. All present swore an oath of loyalty to the nation and to the constitution. There were fireworks on the Pont Neuf, and the statue of Henri IV was decorated with a tricolour scarf.

Over the next few weeks, the journalist William Augustus Miles found the public places of Paris 'inundated with newsvendors and politicians; all ranks of men begin to reason on the principles of government'.[8] The French capital which he had found 'at all times interesting both to the libertine and the philosopher, is more so now than ever', he declared in August 1790, 'and the man who is fond of scrutinizing the human character and of developing the most secret recesses of the heart and mind, will find ample employment for his talents at research, and will discover every moment new matter to excite his admiration or provoke his abhorrence'.[9]

The first few months of the Revolution were months of excitement, optimism, certainly not foreboding; the court ordered fashionable outfits

for the opening of the Estates General, and even court presentations continued into 1790. Yet, by the summer of 1790 the letter pages of the *Chronique de Paris* were urging that distinguishing marks of rank such as expensive 'aristocratic' fashions should be banned and that even the titles from noble tombs should be erased.

Society seemed in a state of hysteria to the young Chateaubriand as he recorded his impressions of the first few months of the Revolution. As he dashed from public ballrooms, to meetings in the Palais Royal, to the gallery of the National Assembly, to the Jacobin club, and through the streets full of self-important hurrying politicians and military men, to theatres where the actors shouted out the latest political news and the people in the pit sang patriotic songs, Paris seemed intoxicated with a heady draught of

---

24 *Satire on the suppression of religious orders*, 1790.

While the monk in his habit is being shaved by an enthusiastic National Guard, the nun contemplates the world of fashionable finery laid before her.

ON ME RAZE AUJOURD'HUI JE ME MARIE DEMAIN &c. A. P. 1790

The old order of society was turned upside down, and was most visibly to be seen in dress: 'Behind a man in a French coat with powdered hair, a sword, a hat carried under his arm, pumps and silk stockings, walked a man wearing his hair short and without powder, an English frock and an American neckcloth'. The shoemaker who measured your foot might be wearing the uniform of the National Guard, and it was a common sight to see (after the confiscation of Church property in 1790) monks reading papers in public houses, and ex-nuns among crowds of frivolous women.[10] Chateaubriand does not enter into details of what such *ci-devant* nuns might wear, but we are told in the pages of the *Journal de la Mode et du Goût* (15 March 1790) that a fashionable outfit was the *robe à la Vestale*, a simple white dress suitable for women returning to society after the convent. The same journal ten days earlier had noted that patriotic zeal was manifest in the range of colourful uniforms adopted by young men of fashion, and Gouverneur Morris, an American lawyer in Paris, was amazed at the fantastic 'military' costumes that had suddenly appeared in the autumn of 1789, each decorated with a tricolour.[11] To those used to the refinement of French formal costume as worn at court, the less showy and sometimes negligent English fashions, adopted by those with egalitarian sympathies, were startling. Mary Berry, in Paris in 1790, and finding it 'at present much in déshabillé', thought the deputies at the National Assembly 'such a set of shabby, ill-dressed, strange-looking people'.[12] Rather more elegant were the versions of English costume seen in the fashion plates, although as interpreted in the flesh by the *élégants*, the results might be surprising, as William Wellesley-Pole, third earl of Mornington found in September 1790, when he noted that such young gentlemen:

in order to show their attachment to the Democracy have sacrificed their curls, toupees and queues; some of them go about with cropped locks like English farmers without any powder, and others wear little black scratch wigs; both these fashions are called Têtes à la Romaine, which is a comical name for such folly . . .[13]

As was customary for a man in his position, he attended court at the Tuileries, and found it a very gloomy occasion; 'many of the young people of the first fashion and rank wear mourning always for economy'.[14] Mourning had always been a fact of life at every court in Europe in the eighteenth century,[15] but it seemed particularly to afflict the French court from 1789 to 1790, with, for example, the death of the Dauphin in June 1789, and the death of the Emperor Joseph II (brother to Marie-Antoinette) in February 1790. Court mourning, with its endless regulations, had a deadening effect on the textile trade, and had long caused resentment; for this reason, and partly because it was a custom linked to court usage, mourning for royalty was curtailed from the summer of 1789. The *Chronique de Paris* (6 December 1789) declared that mourning was a servile custom, and the *Journal de la Mode et du Goût* (25 March 1790), apropos the demise of Joseph II, was pleased to note that little mourning was to be seen, except on a few aristocrats.

Yet it was not only as mourning for royalty that black was worn by some aristocrats; they wore it to mourn for the death of royalty itself, a lament for the diminished powers of the monarchy in France, and a signal of their willingness to die for the royal cause. The *Chronique de Paris* (2 March 1791) recorded an attempt by a band of aristocrats to see the king at the Tuileries, all wearing black, 'pour mourir, disoient-ils, en défendant le roi'; the attempt failed, and the readers of the newspaper were urged to beware of such 'prétendus patriotes'. The *Journal de la Mode et du Goût* (15 April 1790) noted the custom of some 'aristocrates décidés' to wear full mourning as a sign of their total sympathy with royalty. Those who were less attracted towards a monarchical system could wear half-mourning:

25 *Fashion plate*, 1790, from the *Journal de la Mode et du Goût*.

Almost persuaded by the revolutionary cause, this elegant 'demi-converti' wears a scarlet coat, double-breasted and cut very short at the front, while the rest of his outfit is black.

'... jeunes aristocrates ex-nobles, dont le coeur n'est pas encore endurci dans le crime, et qui commencent à se façonner à la constitution Françoise, portent le costume de demi-converti, c'està-dire le demi-deuil'. Such young men, whether really semi-converted to the new constitution or merely prudent, wore, we are told, a scarlet coat, a waistcoat of black cloth or silk, breeches of black casimir (a fine woollen cloth), black stockings and a black cravat (see fig. 25). What was the truly democratic man to wear? According to the first issue of the *Journal de la Mode et du Goût* (25 February 1790), 'un homme vêtu d'un habit de drap noir à la Révolution' wears, with his black cloth coat, a red casimir waistcoat and yellow breeches (although it is equally the fashion, says the magazine, for black breeches to be worn). Black, it seems, was a colour which could be appropriated by all sides of the political spectrum, though it may be possible to make a distinction between silk, as worn by the aristocracy, and the cloth worn by those with 'democratic' sympathies, a tribute to the decreed costume of the Third Estate.

A more direct form of political allegiance can be detected in men's accessories of the period. Boots, for example, indicated a leaning towards democracy, and when shoes were chosen, the tactful man wore either shoe strings or non-precious buckles; gold, silver or jewelled buckles

26 *Fashion plates*, 1789, from the *Magasin des Modes Nouvelles*.

At the top the woman wears a *caraco* and skirt of tricolour-striped satin, inspired by the 'rubans nationaux que les hommes portent à la boutonnière, & dont on fait aussi des cocardes'. On the left of this plate are two buckles, the top one with the towers of the Bastille, and the one underneath a 'boucle au Tiers-Etat'. The plate below shows two 'boucles à la Nation', and in the centre a 'bonnet à la Bastille' shaped like a tower, and trimmed with tricolour ribbon.

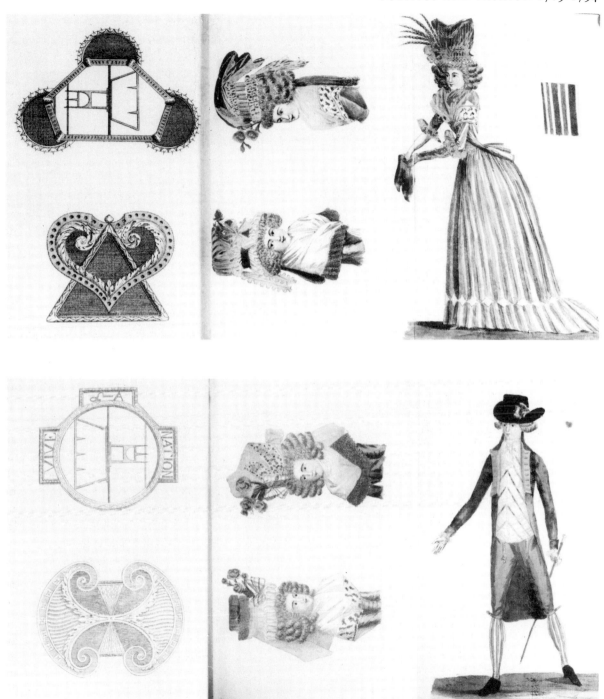

were the sign of the courtier, or at least the man of wealth, and as such the authorities encouraged their donation to the *caisse patriotique* set up in the autumn of 1789.

The truly *à la mode* patriot could wear buckles 'à la Bastille' (shaped in the form of towers) as we read in the *Magasin des Modes Nouvelles* (11 November 1789); alternative fashions were for buckles 'au Tiers-Etat' and 'à la Nation' (*Magasin des Modes*, 1 December 1789) (see fig. 26).

The most obvious homage to recent political events was to wear the tricolour, either in the form of a ribbon in the buttonhole, or – more usually – as a cockade in the hat. The *Magasin des Modes Nouvelles* (21 October 1789) left its male readers in no doubt: 'La cocarde nationale est portée, ou doit l'être, par absolument tous les hommes de la Capitale qui peuvent être en état de porter les armes.' In defiance of the prevailing opinion, some young men voiced their sympathy with the court by wearing white satin cockades inscribed with 'Ludovicus XVI'; this was a reference to the trampling underfoot of the tricolour badge and its replacement by the white Bourbon cockade, by the Flanders regiment on 1 October 1789.[16]

The fashion world, long accustomed to political and social novelties as inspiration for dress, was not slow to respond to the Revolution in terms of women's costume. After an initial flurry of uncertainty around the time of the fall of the Bastille,[17] the *Magasin des Modes Nouvelles* was soon expressing its belief that recent events would be bound to affect dress: 'Il n'y avoit pas de doute qu'une révolution comme celle qui s'opère en France, ne dût fournir à la Capitale l'idée de quelques modes.' (21 September 1789)

Ever since the time of Rose Bertin, headwear had proved to be the most fertile source of topical political comment, a state of affairs which was to gather momentum during the early years of the Revolution. In the issue of the *Magasin des Modes* quoted above, one of the new modes is a hat of white gauze with embroidered olive branches in

green silk, and trimmed with a band of white taffeta on which are embroidered a cross, a sword and a spade and to which is attached a national cockade. It needed no great perception to see that this was clearly symbolic of the union of the three Estates, or 'plutôt la confusion des Ordres (on ne veut plus de ces distinctions en France, il n'y a plus que des Citoyens)'.

27 *Fashion plate*, 1790, from the *Journal de la Mode et du Goût*.

The first issue, dated 25 February 1790, shows a popular style, the skirt and *caraco* jacket. The shoulders are covered with a printed English cotton kerchief.

28 *La marquise de Grécourt*, 1790, Jean-Laurent Mosnier.

In revolutionary times, it is becoming fashionable to dress *à la paysanne*; here the sitter wears a scarf knotted in the form of a cap on her head, and a striped kerchief around her shoulders.

The same magazine, for 1 December 1789, says that it would indeed have been surprising if the *marchandes de modes* had not celebrated the fall of the Bastille, and produces an illustration of a 'bonnet à la Bastille', a confection of white lace and satin, rather like a tower in shape and trimmed with a tricolour ribbon and rosette.

The tricolour, in the form of ribbons, rosettes, and dress materials, was the fashion inspiration for 1789–90; many women, said the *Journal de la Mode et du Goût* (5 March 1790) 'se montrent patriotes, en adoptant les couleurs de la Nation'. Later that month, the couturière Madame Eloffe records that the queen ordered from her 'douze aunes de ruban à la Nation',[18] and at the *Fête de la Fédération* on 14 July, Marie-Antoinette judiciously chose to wear tricolour feathers.

In this particular case, the wearing of tricolour fashions must have been more of a tactful acknowledgement of a popular fashion theme, than an indication of serious political conviction. The fashion magazines, however, made the most of politics as a theme to be exploited. If you wished to show sympathy towards the idea of a new constitution, then you could be seen in a dress of fine Indian muslin embroidered with tiny red, white and blue bouquets (*Journal de la Mode et du Goût*, 15 April 1790) (see fig. 29); if, on the other hand, you supported the clergy who had refused to take an oath of loyalty to the constitution, you could choose 'un costume . . . catholique, ou à l'évêque non-jureur' which consisted of a red and black *pierrot* jacket, a white linen skirt 'en rochet', and a bonnet of black trimmed with gold, pearls, diamonds and an aigrette of white feathers (*Journal de la Mode et du Goût*, 5 February 1792) (see fig. 30). Jacket and skirt styles were particularly associated with a functional simplicity, and therefore suitable for the fashionable democrat; the *Journal de la Mode et du Goût* (5 December 1790) describes a *pierrot* and skirt of 'feuille-morte' satin, a white gauze fichu and matching 'bonnet à l'américaine', adding, 'ce déshabillé s'appelle à la democrate'.

29 *Fashion plate*, 1790, from the *Journal de la Mode et du Goût*.

This, we are told, is a fashionable woman 'vêtue à la constitution'; her dress is of fine cotton patterned with tiny tricolour bouquets, over which is worn a 'fichu en chemise'. A faintly martial air is created by the hat, a 'demi-casque' of black gauze with a red ribbon and aigrette.

30 *Fashion plate*, 1792, from the *Journal de la Mode et du Goût*.

Those who wish to demonstrate their loyalty to the non-juring clergy, can adopt 'un costume . . . catholique, ou à l'évêque non-jureur'. This consists of a red and black striped *pierrot* jacket, a red and black shawl, and a linen skirt 'en rochet'; the bonnet is of black satin with a white gold-trimmed ribbon, and a white aigrette.

Equally seen as democratic were the fashionable French versions of English *redingotes* and riding habits; they had the right connotations of informality and martial vigour. The *Magasin des Modes Nouvelles* for 11 September 1789 voiced the general view that 'nous sommes devenus tous soldats'. The *Journal de la Mode et du Goût* (possibly inspired by the uniform of the National Guard) promoted the 'femme patriote' in 'une redingote nationale de drap fin bleu de roi', edged with red braid, and worn with a white linen skirt (25 March 1790). Later that year, we are shown a 'femme patriote avec le nouvel uniforme', who wears a blue riding habit, faced with red, a white dimity *gilet*, and a black hat with the ubiquitous cockade (25 August) (see fig. 31).

Although women were urged to show their patriotic zeal by wearing native fabrics of comparative simplicity (the *Chronique de Paris*, for example, in its edition of 9 October 1789, urged women of fashion to wear French woollen stuffs to inspire 'toutes les femmes patriotes'), the fashion magazines show far more silks and expensive Indian muslins, than cheaper materials such as plain wool and printed cotton. The ensembles in the *Journal* do not conform, even when they claim to be 'democratic', to our notion of what revolutionary toilettes should be, and they look particularly showy when set against the simplicity of, say, the costumes portrayed by David in his portraits of fashionable ladies in 1790-1. This paradox can partly be explained by a deliberate desire on the part of the artist to subdue intrusive details of fashion which might detract from the character of the sitter, or a tactful decision, in a time of great social and political stress, on the part of the sitter to be portrayed in a simple, informal costume. For there is no doubt that women continued to have an absorbing interest in high fashion even in a time of political upheaval. Addressing this curious fact, the *Journal de la Mode et du Goût* (15 April 1791) found that among 'les gens de qua-

59

31 *Fashion plate*, from the *Journal de la Mode et du Goût*, 25 August 1790.

The 'femme patriote avec le nouvel uniforme' demonstrates her revolutionary enthusiasm in a jacket and skirt of dark blue faced with red, worn with a white cotton *gilet*; the tricolour motif is also seen in her cockade. Her hair is unpowdered and simple in style, a deliberate contrast to the curled and powdered coiffures of high fashion.

lité', women have most to lose; they do not, of course, have a profession or political vocation and recent changes in society have deprived them of the pleasures of ceremony and the consolation of titles; as it not very likely that they will turn exclusively to the joys of domesticity, dress assumes an even greater importance in their lives. Increasingly, however, real luxury in dress was on the wane. 'Le luxe tombe, s'écrient les marchands; déjà l'or et l'argent ne sont plus employés dans la parure'; this comment by the *Journal de la Mode et du Goût* (25 June 1790) is an acknowledgement of the changing tastes of the times. Patriotic women had given their jewellery to the government and in its place they had chosen to wear simpler semi-precious items, or deliberately non-precious jewels, often with political significance; Madame de Genlis (who had renounced her titles to become Citizeness Brûlart) ordered, to go with her dress trimmed with tricolour ribbons, a locket made of a bit of stone taken from the Bastille.[19] When the *Journal de la Mode et du Goût* (5 June 1790) advertised a ring which some women were wearing in the form of a gold sphere enamelled in blue, white and gold, inscribed with the words 'La Nation, la Loi, et le Roi', it did so apologetically, saying that such a jewel was worn out of patriotism, not luxury, in the hope that, with this credo, the French people could be united.

In spite of the pious hope expressed by many well-wishers that some form of constitutional

32 *La marquise d'Orvilliers*, 1790, Jacques-Louis David.

Slightly self-conscious under the penetrating eye of the artist, Madame d'Orvilliers wears a plain black silk dress over a white muslin bodice; the red silk sash at her waist echoes the bandeau in her lightly powdered hair. The whole effect is softened by a black silk mantle edged with embroidered net, which drapes over her arm, and the back of her seat.

monarchy could at least keep the king on the throne, albeit with reduced powers, the situation by 1791 was sliding out of moderate control, exacerbated by the death of Mirabeau in April of that year. In June the royal family, virtual prisoners in the Tuileries, tried to flee abroad but were stopped at Varennes, and brought back in humiliation to Paris. From this time the king lost all political credibility, and there were growing calls for a republic. Among the groups respon-

sible was the Cordeliers club (founded by Danton in 1790) which organized a petition demanding the abdication of Louis XVI; the crowd gathering to sign it in the Champ de Mars on 17 July was fired on by the National Guard led by Lafayette, and some fifty people were killed.

The Cordeliers club, along with the Jacobin club, supported the increasing band of radical, republican deputies who were elected in September 1791 to the new Legislative Assembly, and who were called the 'Mountain', from the raised seats they occupied at one end of the hall; this group, the Jacobins, had Paris as their main power base. The largest group in the Assembly were the Girondins, moderate republicans whose strength lay in the provinces (a number of their leaders came from Bordeaux in the *département* of the Gironde); there was also a moderate-sized group called the Feuillants (they included men like Sieyès and Lafayette whose initial Jacobin sympathies had waned in proportion to the growth of extremism in the left), who were the

33 *'La Promenade Publique'*, 1792 Philibert-Louis Debucourt.

Here, in the gardens of the Palais-Egalité (formerly the Palais-Royal) the fashionable world continues to amuse itself regardless of the collapse of the monarchy. Under the chestnut trees, fashionable courtesans (in the centre) mingle with elegant dandies, and on the right a little waiter carrying ice-creams from the café de Foy stands beside a group of elderly men seated at a table discussing the latest news from the war front.

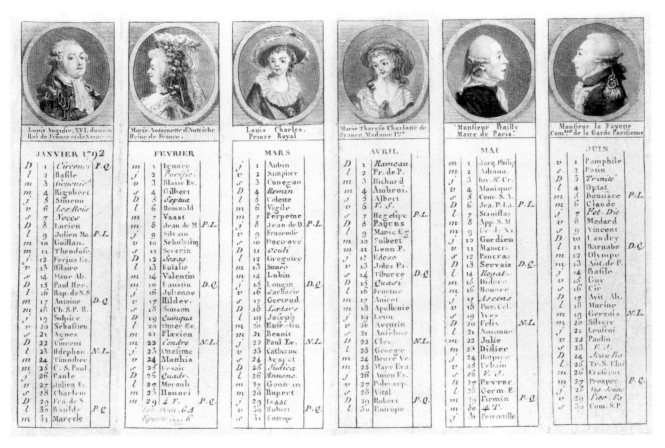

34 *Almanac for 1792 – January to June.*

In accordance with tradition, the King, Queen and royal children are depicted here, but a sign of the times is the presence of important political figures like 'Monsieur Bailly, Maire de Paris', and 'Monsieur la Fayette Com^dant de la Garde Parisienne'.

most supportive (albeit in a lukewarm way) of the idea of a constitutional monarchy.

There were, by the summer of 1791, very few outright supporters of the monarchy. The king's brothers, the comte d'Artois and the comte de Provence, had fled, as had many aristocrats; in Paris coats of arms on carriages and over doorways were erased, and newspapers like the *Journal de Paris* advertised the luxury goods and chattels of the departed nobility. Many of the *émigrés* gathered in Koblenz, some fifty miles from the French frontier at the meeting of the Rhine and the Moselle, under the wing of the Elector of Trèves, uncle of Louis XVI, in despair at the turn of events in France.

During 1792, the pace of change quickened as the *ancien régime* dissolved, giving way to a new society roughly hewn from a mixture of revolutionary ideals and war-time exigencies. Returning to Paris in 1792, Chateaubriand found the mood very different; the people were no longer 'tumultuous, curious, eager', but 'threatening' and determined to push 'the old world into the background'.[20] In the summer of that year, the old world took a further knock as elections to the

35 *Louis XVI drinks a toast to the Revolution*, 20 June 1792, Pierre Gabriel Berthault.

Dressed formally in an embroidered silk suit, and with the *cordon bleu* of the Saint-Esprit, a *bonnet rouge* is placed somewhat incongruously on the King's powdered bag wig as he is forced to drink to the success of the Revolution.

36 *Cockade reputedly worn by Louis XVI at his trial, December 1792.*

This cockade, of red, white and blue silk with tarnished silver-gilt thread, was, according to the inscription, worn by Louis XVI 'during his mock trial before the Ruffians calling themselves the National Convention'.

37 *'Le 10 août 1792'*, François Gérard.

After the attack on the royal apartments in the Tuileries on 10 August, the King and his family fled to the Legislative Assembly, where they were put behind bars for their own safety. The Assembly officials recoil before the dramatic entry of the *sans-culottes*, who demand the deposition of the monarchy. Gérard was later commissioned by the Convention to record this event, but the work was never completed; this is one of the sketches that survives.

Symbolically trampling underfoot the plundered regalia of royalty, the heroic *sans-culottes* in their unrealistically elegant trousers which almost imitate classical nudity, point accusing fingers at the royal family in their cage. Some of the *sans-culottes* and their supporters carry trophies from their encounter with the Swiss guards at the Tuileries; others hoist aloft the *bonnet rouge*, symbol of the triumph of the people over the vestiges of royal despotism.

National Convention returned an almost entirely republican assembly, with further Jacobin gains in Paris. As the various parties struggled for supremacy, the Girondins became the party of the right, and the left[21] included Danton, Robespierre, Saint-Just, plus a few *ci-devant* nobles like Barras and Philippe-Egalité.

Time was running out for the monarchy. On 20 June a crowd marched into the Tuileries and compelled Louis to wear the *bonnet rouge*; on 10 August (a day which was to become sacrosanct to ardent republicans) the *sans-culottes* and their supporters, in despair at the failure of the government to depose the monarchy, invaded and pillaged the royal palace, massacred many of the Swiss guards, and forced the royal family to take refuge in the *manège*. This event, greeted with horror all over Europe, marked the beginning of extremism in politics; the monarchy was deposed, and armies sent by Austria and Prussia (with whom France had been at war since the spring of 1792) invaded France. August 1792 saw a popular rising by the *commune* of Paris, to be followed by massacres in the French prisons in early September, carried out by some *sections* who claimed that counter-revolutionary intrigue was being plotted; this first Terror signalled the gradual eclipse of the Girondins and the virtual take-over of the government by the Jacobins, supported by the *sans-culottes*.

In a tense atmosphere of waiting and watching, of suspicion and barely suppressed hysteria, what were people conveying by their clothing? How did they indicate in the language of dress the dangerous spirit of the times?

The times were troubled, in particular, for those who were noble or connected by ties of occupation or sympathy to the now deposed monarchy. In a situation where the monarchy and aristocracy were identified with treacherous allegiance to countries hostile to France, it was obviously dangerous to appear too elegant and stylish in dress. Madame Tussaud in 1792 saw Philippe-Egalité in 'a short jacket, pantaloons and a round hat, with a handkerchief worn sailor-fashion loose round the neck, with the ends long and hanging down, the shirt collar seen above ... the hair cut short without powder à la Titus, and shoes tied with strings'.[22] This elegant affectation of working-class clothing was part of the perilous game that the *ci-devant* duc d'Orléans was playing in the summer of 1792 to counteract the disadvantage of having been nobly born. The defeats suffered by the disorganized French army encouraged popular fury against the crown and the aristocracy, a fever fanned by the Jacobins and also by the ferocious politician-cum-journalist Jean Paul Marat with his paper *L'Ami du Peuple*.

Once the realities of war were brought home to the people of France, the playful enthusiasm for military attire, which had influenced men's fashions in the first months of the Revolution, disappeared. The *émigré* regiments were mocked for their luxurious uniforms; 'habits à la Cob-

38 *A young man of fashion*, Pierre-Alexandre Wille.

Dating from the early 1790s, this drawing by an artist with revolutionary sympathies shows a foppish young man whose stylish cut-away coat is adorned with huge oval buttons, almost matching in size the Artois buckles on his shoes. The slouched round hat (an English style) is adorned with a tricolour cockade. He carries a 'Hercules' club, a twisted stick, which is not just a fashionable accessory, but a weapon of defence in case of street brawls arising out of political differences.

39 *'Incroyable' doll*, early 1790s.

This puppet *muscadin* with his outrageously large starched cravat is otherwise dressed in the height of elegance with striped coat and knee-breeches, bicorne hat, and black pumps.

lentz' – described by the *Chronique de Paris* (29 July 1791) as 'Habit bleu, revers & paremens jaunes, veste rouge, pantalon chamois, bottines à la houzarde, sabre, quatre pistolets, épaulette & aiguillette pour les officiers, bouton jaune avec trois fleurs de lys' – were the sort of Ruritanian outfits worn by toy soldiers, or by counter-revolutionary *élégants* masquerading as martial. The same sentiment is expressed in the pages of the *Journal de la Mode et du Goût* (5 October 1791): 'Depuis quelques temps nos jeunes gens se sont transformés en Hercules, et c'est une chose plaisante de voir leur foible bras traîner une lourde massue qui jusqu' à présent ne leur a servi qu' à tuer des mouches et à faire peur aux enfans.' Such an effeminate, trailing his club, betrays his royalist sympathies by wearing 'un habit d'automne de drap de Silésie, couleur des cheveux de la reine', a lace cravat, and an elaborately curled coiffure. Earlier that year, in the same journal, we find 'un jeune homme costumé à la contre-révolution', in a black coat, yellow *gilet* and green breeches (25 May 1791) (see fig. 40); the counter-revolutionary elements are possibly indicated by the colour green (worn by the supporters of the 'plus royaliste que le roi' comte d'Artois), and the powdered hair.

It appears that most men who supported the Revolution wore their hair cut short and unpowdered. A popular style derived from the role of Titus as played by the great actor Talma in Voltaire's *Brutus*, on 30 May 1791 (the anniversary of the author's death): 'Huit jours après, tous les jeunes gens de Paris avaient les cheveux coupés courts et de cette soirée data la mode de coiffer à la Titus'.[23]

Apart from differences in coiffure which might help to distinguish one political viewpoint from another, masculine costume as seen in the pages of the fashion plates seems fairly uniform, consisting as it does of elegant versions of English country clothing. With regard to the more formal styles, the *Journal de la Mode et du Goût* (5 February 1792) despaired of any change: 'Ce sont

40 *Fashion plate*, 1791, from the *Journal de la Mode et du Goût*.

This young man, 'costumé à la contre-révolution', is difficult to distinguish from his equally elegant contemporaries with pro-revolutionary sentiments. However, the green casimir breeches may indicate support for the cause of the comte d'Artois, and his cravat is edged with black, possible testimony to mourning for the threatened demise of the monarchy.

41 *Fashion plate*, 1792, from the *Journal de la Mode et du Goût*.

Under the influence of English sporting costume, this young gentleman wears a cloth coat, casimir breeches imitating leather, and English boots. Those who adopt this style, says the *Journal*, 'ont toujours l'air de descendre de cheval, ou d'être prêts à y monter'.

toujours des culottes sans fond, qui montent par-dessus les hanches, et si étroites, qu'elles ne permettent pas de faire la moindre enjambée . . . Les habits, pour la plupart, sont bruns ou noirs, les redingotes de plus mauvais goût; les gilets presque tous rouges.'

Out of doors, says the *Journal* for 1 June 1792 (see fig. 41), men wear tailcoats, high-crowned hats, boots and they carry a cane; they look as if they have just got down from a horse, or are about to mount one. Functional simplicity was the keynote of male dress, which was sometimes carried to extremes in a determination to indicate a sympathy with republicanism. Dr John Moore, in Paris in the autumn of 1792, noted 'a great affectation of that plainness in dress and simplicity of expression which are supposed to belong to Republicans'; he met 'a young man of one of the first families in France . . . a violent democrate', attending the theatre 'in boots, his hair cropt and his whole dress slovenly; on this being taken notice of, he said "That he was accustoming himself to appear like a Republican"'.[24]

During the Terror in particular, it was politically suspect to appear elegant; at best it implied a greater concern with one's appearance than with the benefit of people in general, and at worst it could be taken as almost a presumption of treason. Helen Maria Williams, a Francophile with republican inclinations, while rejoicing (in 1791) that personal vanity was on the wane, discovered (in 1793) that even cleanliness was counter-revolutionary: 'The obsolete term of muscadin, which means a scented fop, was revived; and every man who had the boldness to appear in a clean shirt was branded with that appellation . . .'.[25] And yet, she notes, Robespierre 'always appeared not only dressed with neatness, but with some degree of elegance, and while he called himself the leader of the sans-culottes, never adopted the costume of his band'.[26] Madame Tussaud remembered his gallantry towards ladies, and his fondness for dress; he preferred to wear silk, his hair was powdered, and

he was particularly fussy about arranging his neckcloth and shirt frill in front of the mirror.[27]

Robespierre's sartorial tastes meant that elegance in dress was not totally abandoned even during the Terror, even though it was a minority preference. A free people, claimed one writer in April 1794, must not confuse elegance with luxury: 'Le luxe n'est point le goût, et en dépit des pantalons, des bonnets rouges, des cheveux coupés et des moustaches, il est permis à des républicains de porter d'élégantes culottes, des chapeaux d'une forme heureuse, une chevelure où brille la main délicate et légère du perruquier . . .'.[28]

Any discussion of the merits of fashion might have been a welcome diversion from the terrifying events which engulfed France after the downfall of the monarchy. Within a few weeks of the execution of Louis XVI, in January 1793, France was at war with most of Europe; the new republic also had to face internal unrest in the form of uprisings (encouraged by *émigrés* and with help from hostile nations), of which the most sustained was that in the Vendée in the spring and summer. It was partly the military reverses suffered by France in the spring of 1793 which helped to sweep the Girondins from office and to make Robespierre the virtual ruler of France. Maximilien de Robespierre, son and grandson of lawyers and a lawyer himself, was elected to represent Arras in 1789. Gradually working his way to become master of the Paris revolutionary machine, he joined the Committee of Public Safety in July 1793. This committee (which had been created in the spring of 1793) was officially responsible to the Convention, but really dominated it; it directed war and diplomacy, the other major committee (that of General Security) being the chief organ of the

---

42 *Maximilien de Robespierre*, François Gérard.

A sketch drawn from life during a sitting of the Convention shows Robespierre dressed with his habitual elegance.

les yeux verts le teint pâle, habit nankin rayé vert,
gilet blanc rayé bleu, cravatte blanche rayée rouge.
(croquis d'après nature à une séance de la Convention

43 *Camille Desmoulins in Prison*, 1794, Hubert Robert.

Gazing at a portrait of his young wife, the revolutionary orator and journalist wears a slim-fitting greatcoat, striped *gilet*, and light breeches; on his feet are soft indoor shoes. The hat (of fur or sheepskin) is worn for warmth and to denote intellectual kinship with Rousseau, whose famous portrait in 'Armenian' costume (by Allan Ramsay, 1766) includes such a form of headwear.

The artist (who was himself imprisoned during the Terror, but who – unlike Desmoulins – survived) depicts with a sympathetic eye the homely details of domestic life bounded by the walls of a small cell. Desmoulins' washing implements and crockery are on a shelf over the bed, and on the wall underneath are pegs for his clothes – a cloak, a cockaded hat, and a printed cotton kerchief. The drawstring cloth bag hanging on a nail probably contains other items of clothing such as linen.

revolutionary police and the administration of revolutionary justice in the provinces.

It was Robespierre's idea to purge France of corruption by the rule of Terror which lasted from the autumn of 1793 until his downfall the following July. In March 1793 the Revolutionary Tribunal had come into being to try counter-revolutionary activity, with death the increasingly frequent sentence. In the same month all *émigrés* were declared legally dead, and their property confiscated. The Law of Suspects (17 September 1793) authorized the revolutionary committees in each *section* of Paris to investigate and detain suspects, often on the most flimsy pretexts. The daily journal of the Convention, *La Révolution de 92 ou Journal de la Convention*, grimly records the crimes of the 'gens suspects'; the aristocrats (and their sympathizers), the money merchants, the agitators and the 'prêtres réfractaires', among others, and comments (14 July 1794) 'chaque jour la tête de quelque nouveau conspirateur tombe sous le glaive vengeur des loix'. One of these 'conspirators', in spite of his avowed republicanism and the fact that he had voted for the death of the king, was Philippe-Egalité, guillotined just a few weeks after Marie-Antoinette, in the autumn of 1793. Before the French Revolution, only prisoners of noble birth had the right to be beheaded; in the Terror, in a grim extension of the principle of equality, the humanitarian invention of Dr Joseph Guillotin ended prolonged pain, and enabled a much quicker rate of execution. Under Robespierre's 'crystalline conviction of rightness', a nightmare climate of fear, bloodshed and destruction hung over France, which became, said Madame Roland, writing in prison in 1793, 'a vast Golgotha of carnage, an arena of horrors, where her children tear and destroy each other'. Given such a fearful situation, how far could we expect the feminine arts of fashion to survive?

Looking at the formerly undisputed leader of fashion, Marie-Antoinette, we find her changed circumstances reflected in her expenditure on

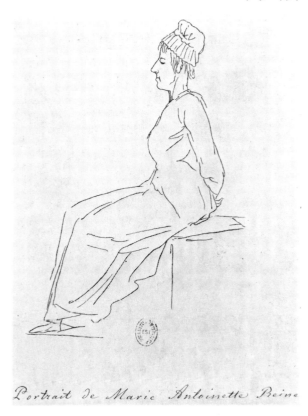

Portrait de Marie Antoinette Reine

44 *Marie-Antoinette on her way to execution*, 1793, Jacques-Louis David.

From a window in a house on the rue Saint-Honoré, David sketched Marie-Antoinette on her way to the scaffold. Unrecognizable as the former queen of France once so fashionably dressed, but here with a kind of bedraggled dignity which even David was forced to acknowledge, Marie-Antoinette wears a loose white morning gown, and a starched cap over her hair cut short in readiness for the blade of the guillotine.

clothing, from the lavish amounts (often over 100,000 livres per annum) of the early and mid 1780s, to the relatively small sums of about 36,000 and 18,000 livres in 1791 and 1792 respectively.[29]

By 1791, the queen's once-praised beauty had

45 *La marquise de Pastoret and her son, c.* 1792, Jacques-Louis David.

In a society in which obvious signs of aristocratic caste are increasingly tactless, if not downright dangerous, the marquise is depicted simply as a mother in understated clothing, a plain chemise gown with a carelessly arranged kerchief. Hairstyles elaborately curled and powdered are also unfashionable in an egalitarian world, and the sitter's hair, half out of curl, shows little sign of attention from a fashionable coiffeur.

vanished under the stress of political reverses and her hair had turned grey.[30] A virtual prisoner in the Tuileries, and after 10 August 1792, a real prisoner in the Temple (once the headquarters of the Knights Templars), she needed fewer clothes, and those of the simpler sort, as there was no longer a court with glittering ceremonial to preside over. In any case, when the Tuileries was sacked by the mob on 10 August, the royal wardrobe was ransacked and 'everyone sought to decorate his or her person with some fragment of the devastation';[31] what was left of the royal wardrobe was later sold.

No longer queen, but 'la femme Capet', Marie-Antoinette nevertheless had a sizeable wardrobe in the early days of her imprisonment; in the summer of 1792 we find her ordering items like bonnets, mantles, fichus etc. from Rose Bertin. Bertin's last invoice to her famous client is dated 5 October 1792, by which time the modiste was in Koblenz, having decided that a safer and more lucrative existence would be to sell her expertise to an *émigrée* clientele; she took with her four of her famous dressed dolls, and fifteen cases of 'des étoffes, des soieries, des velours, des dentelles, des plumes, des rubans ...'.[32] In the Temple, the royal ladies (the king's sister Madame Elisabeth was also imprisoned there) spent their time reading, teaching the royal children, and mending clothes, now very much diminished; one of the tasks imposed by their

gaolers was to unpick the crowns from the royal linen which was sent in to them.[33] In a faint echo of the formal changes in toilette which had been part of a courtly existence, the queen at midday replaced her white cotton morning gown with a patterned brown linen dress.[34]

Such a custom was not only a remembrance of happier times past, but a sign of self-respect, all the more necessary in the deadening uniformity of a prison existence. During the Terror, many aristocratic women were imprisoned, along with those whom the Law of Suspects deemed to be so because of their behaviour, manners and associates. Records and letters show how important it was for them to keep up appearances,[35] and an interest in fashion could not only help to ameliorate a prison existence, but could signal defiance to the political authorities; some women found the resources somehow to wear three changes of clothing a day, and those with fewer clothes spent much of their time mending and washing them.[36]

It was clear, even in the months leading up to the Terror, that the very concept of fashion was under attack, implying, as it did, a fairly idle existence centred around rapid and expensive changes in style. The spirit of the times was not in sympathy with the arts of fashion, and in the autumn of 1791 Gouverneur Morris noted the exodus of modistes from Paris;[37] the absence of their expertise in the trimming of dress in particular may have contributed to the vogue for simpler styles, seen both in portraiture and in fashion plates.

The *Journal de la Mode et du Goût* during 1791 and 1792 records how the overcast mood in politics and society is reflected in dress. Simplicity in dress is fashionable, as well as a corresponding sobriety in manners; it is no longer the vogue, comments the issue of 10 May 1792, to have 'un air riant, mol & folâtre', but to have 'un ton décidé, la tête haute, la démarche ferme, un peu moins de babil ...'.

Formality in dress was the exception rather

75

than the rule, as society itself became inward-looking; it was often safer, in fact, to be at home and not outside where an injudicious choice of dress might occasion the wrath of the people. 'Un air sévère' was particularly worn by 'les femmes de distinction', noted the *Journal* in one of its last issues early in 1793; such women also had to avoid clothes that looked as though they needed careful manipulation and complicated movements and were of manifestly expensive fabrics – these things were the sign of a hated aristocratic caste. It seems at times that the *Journal* tempts Providence in advertising items of dress with aristocratic names, a coiffure 'à la Coblentz' (1 March 1792), a 'pouf à la reine' of white linen decorated with royal blue marguerites (1 June 1792), or a 'robe à la reine' of white taffeta (1 August 1792). After 10 August, such fashions would have been dangerous rather than tactless, in the prevailing republican mood. The shops were full of goods with armorial bearings; ex-noble carriages with their coats of arms obliterated by clouds painted on the sides stood on cab ranks, and it was even, according to one visitor, proposed to abolish the titles of chessmen.[38]

In a climate where 'monsieur' and 'madame' were replaced, in the autumn of 1792, by 'citoyen' and 'citoyenne', we would expect to find egalitarianism expressed in what high fashion remained. From the fashion plates we can see that the most common everyday attire is a jacket and skirt; slightly more formal is a 'robe économique' or 'demi-parure', which, as the name implies, took less fabric than the formal open robe reserved only for exceptional occasions such as weddings. Hair is generally unpowdered, and simple kerchiefs often take the place of more elaborate head-dresses.

The style of dress closest to that worn by working women was the jacket and skirt. It is this costume, in printed cotton, with a matching shawl, which the *Journal de la Mode et du Goût* (20 November 1792) (see fig. 46) declares to be born out of the new republican government; such a

46 *Fashion plate*, 1792, from the *Journal de la Mode et du Goût*.

This bonnet, kerchief, *pierrot* jacket and skirt are made of printed cotton. The *tout ensemble* is a costume 'à l'égalité'.

costume, 'à l'égalité', was worn with a printed linen head-dress, 'très à la mode parmi les Républicaines'. One suspects, however, that fashionable women, even those with impeccable republican convictions, chose dress because it was stylish rather than for its political significance. Thus, Madame Roland appeared elegant in prison with her 'white English muslin trimmed with blonde, with a black velvet sash'[39] and Charlotte Corday, at her trial for the murder of Marat in July 1793, was admired in her spotted Indian muslin dress, rose-coloured fichu, and a tall black hat trimmed with green ribbons.[40]

Both the fashion magazines and the records of Barbier's silk business indicate that cottons and linens were not the only fabrics worn; Barbier continued to supply lightweight silks such as taffeta to his fashionable customers, the most popular colours being black and white.[41] Combinations of red, white and blue, worn so enthusiastically in the early months of the Revolution, were no longer so popular; neither, it seems, was the promotion of grey as a 'moderate' colour by the *Journal de la Mode et du Goût* (15 January 1792) which urged that dress should not be seen as a battleground for political beliefs.

Whatever the costume worn, a tricolour cockade was compulsory for women from 21 September 1793; although silk cockades were available, these were sometimes torn off by the 'femmes du peuple', who preferred their fellow-citizens to wear large woollen ones.[42] True republican women were supposed to wear simple jewellery (Jacobin pamphlets urged women to be adorned just in virtue) in the form of ornaments commemorating the Revolution. According to one account, the executions of the Terror gave jewellers a new source of inspiration – 'women and young girls wore golden and silver guillotines in pins and brooches and combs, even in ear-rings'.[43]

'Malgré la guerre, nos troubles intestins, les mouvemens politiques de toute l'Europe, &c, le goût des femmes pour la parure est aussi vif que jamais', was the slightly desperate comment by

36. Cahier 1793.

47 *Fashion plate*, 1793, from the *Journal de la Mode et du Goût*.

From one of the last issues of the *Journal*. '. . . une aimable simplicité règne aujourd' hui . . .' – a linen bonnet, and a simple robe of lilac taffeta.

48 *A musical evening in a salon*, 1793, Jean-Baptiste Mallet.

Fashionable society continues to amuse itself in spite of – or perhaps because of – the downfall of the monarchy. These stylish *élégants* could have stepped out of the pages of the *Journal de la Mode et du Goût*.

the *Journal de la Mode et du Goût* (1 February 1793) shortly before it closed down. From then onwards, and particularly during the Terror, it is difficult to assess how much there was in the way of fashion, and, since fashion exists by example and communication, how it might have been transmitted. Although 'society' in the sense of a court-dominated hierarchy had gone, there were enough fashionable women with an interest, at least, in the elegant, simple styles seen in the pages of the *Journal*, to ensure that the momentum of

fashion kept on during 1793–4. Although Morris maintained that Paris was at 'the mercy of the provinces for its fashions',[44] there were enough modistes in the capital to supply the less exalted taste of republican ladies. As travel was often difficult (and it might have been embarrassing to be seen visiting a modiste) a postal service could be offered. In April 1792 the editor of the *Journal de la Mode et du Goût* advertised a service whereby the costumes illustrated in his magazine could be supplied by post to ladies if they would send their measurements; the list of outfits included 'robes économiques' (offered in striped satin or *chiné* taffeta for 100 livres, and in linen or muslin for 80 livres), 'négligés', i.e. *caracos/pierrots* and skirts (costing 100 livres for silk, and 80 livres for linen, muslin or gauze), and linen shawls from 24 to 40 livres.[45]

During the Terror, the *Journal de Paris* for 19

October 1793 carried a supplement, advertising the wide range of costume offered by a dressmaker, 'Citoyenne Raspal, ci-devant Teillard' of the 'ci-devant Palais Royal'. The details of the costumes listed do not conjure up a picture of republican austerity, but the reverse, with satin *redingotes* and *douillettes*, pelisses trimmed with swansdown, and a variety of robes and all-in-one gowns. Among the last-mentioned is a chemise 'à la Républicaine', buttoned down the front and with a Roman belt fastened at the side; it cost 190 livres in silk, and 120 livres in muslin, striped gauze or linen.[46]

Citizeness Raspal also offered a selection of hats and bonnets, again rather surprising as hats in particular were thought of during the Terror as aristocratically frivolous; Georges Duval remembered that 'le chapeau, qu'il fût de paille ou de soie, avait été déclaré contre-révolutionnaire'.[47]

Laure Junot, on the other hand, recollected that elegant items of clothing were safe enough for news to be hidden in them: 'News was frequently sent from Paris to the country in the lining of a coat, the crown of a hat, or a box of artificial flowers ... My mother was sometimes very reluctant to pull to pieces the beautiful articles of millinery which came from Paris in this way.'[48] Whether the future duchesse d'Abrantès' mother used the postal service offered by Citizeness Raspal, is not clear, but the latter's dressmaking business prospered. Advertised in the *Journal de Paris* (31 October 1794), many of the ensembles are classical in theme – a chemise 'à la Grecque', 'bonne pour le lever & l'appartement', a 'robe et jupe à la Romaine', a 'robe ronde à la Diane', and so on.[49]

By this time, the Terror was over, and it becomes possible once more, albeit haltingly at first, to follow the course of fashion.

3 | Brave New World: People and State 1789–1794

It is perhaps a paradox that in spite of the class warfare which marked the course (and the aftermath) of the French Revolution, one of its great aspirations was a sense of nationhood. Almost from the very first it was the 'people's' revolution; a wholly new sense of the cultural identity of the working class – its language, dress and manner of living – were brought to the fore by the events of 1789 and, even more, after the downfall of the monarchy in the autumn of 1792. As with all questions of class, however, we enter a minefield of misunderstanding and confusion; who were the 'people' and who was to speak for them? Do we mean the mass of the apolitical poor, or the quasi-politicized *sans-culottes* whose clamour for radical reform was mixed with a need for food, causing spontaneous riots which occasionally ran counter to the interests of their bourgeois allies, the Jacobins? The Jacobins themselves, the real intellectual inspiration of the Revolution, and on the whole middle class, also aimed to speak for the people, and from the autumn of 1792 they had become all-powerful.

Taken up into government, they sought a secular society based on social equality, with the kind of ruthless and violent efficiency indicated by Chamfort's aside, 'Sois mon frère, ou je te tue,' a chilling reminder of Jacobin ethics, which in his case proved fatal. Against a background of internal dissent and external hostility, they carried through one of the most profound revolutions in history, not just with regard to politics, but in modes of life and ways of thinking. Men and women found their lives radically changed at every level. Not only were they all caught up in the war effort,[1] but they found their very existence transformed by a series of social and cultural reforms from 1792 onwards. These included the introduction of civil marriage and divorce,[2] a new calendar, and a new currency;[3] their very surroundings, the streets they lived in, and the churches they had been familiar with since childhood, were renamed and reconsecrated to a new republican way of life.

The guiding force behind these changes was the Jacobin club (which had its origins in a club for the Breton deputies to the Estates-General in 1789); it soon expanded into the *Société des Amis de la Constitution* which by 1792 had thousands of branches throughout the provinces. The idea of a political club also derived from the literary and masonic societies of the eighteenth century; from the late autumn of 1789, 'the earnest talkers of the literary and patriotic societies throughout the

---

49 *Le Mariage Républicain et le Divorce Républicain, c.* 1794, Jean-Baptiste Mallet.

In the marriage scene, a statue of Hymen holding a torch blesses the couple with a nuptial crown, as the mayor, wearing his tricolour sash and Phrygian bonnet, congratulates them; on the right the details are recorded and witnessed by family members. The bridal couple are very elegantly dressed, she in a silk dress, lace-edged kerchief, and elaborately trimmed bonnet, he in powdered hair, tight-fitting tailored suit and low-heeled pumps. The subsequent divorce (Hymen's torch is out and she holds the broken bonds of marriage) shows the acrimony both between the couple, and the family members forced to take sides and to arrange the financial settlements. Still elegantly dressed, but more casual, the wife wears a cotton gown with plain crossover kerchief, and the husband is now in undressed, unpowdered hair, pantaloons and boots.

50 *A Revolutionary Committee under the Terror*, 1793–4, engraved by Pierre Gabriel Berthault after Alexandre-Evariste Fragonard from *Tableaux Historiques de la Révolution Française*, 1817.

The humble stance of the petitioning family on the left is contrasted with the casual, slovenly indifference of some members of the revolutionary committee, and the violent gestures of others. The elegantly dressed middle-class petitioner in his tailored coat and round hat is deliberately contrasted with the open-necked shirts, short jackets and *bonnets rouges* of the militant revolutionaries.

country began to realise that France was theirs to govern'.[4] Through their power base in the former library of the old Dominican convent off the rue St Honoré, and their network of affiliated *sociétés populaires*, the Jacobins were an effective organization for lobbying public support towards their political aim of a Jacobin republic; during their most effective year, 1794, it has been estimated that there were about half a million members in France.[5]

It was the high moral tone and the serious Puritan element in their thinking, that led inexorably to the Terror of 1793–4; 'La folie de la Révolution fut de vouloir instituer la vertu sur la terre. Quand on veut rendre les hommes bons et sages, libres, modérés, généreux, on est amené fatalement à vouloir les tuer tous.'[6] A feeling that liberty and luxury were incompatible led the Jacobin government to admire and emulate the austere virtues of ancient Rome, rather than the more seductive charms of classical Greece. Not only did they commission David to design state

Les Tricoteuses Jacobines, ou de Robespierre.

*Elles étoient un grand nombre à qui l'on donnoit
40 Sols par jour pour aller dans la tribune des Jacobins
applaudir les motions révolutionnaires.*

An 2.

JACOBIN *vociférant une
Motion à la Tribune.*

LE BONET ROUGE.

*Beaucoup de Citoyens craignans d'être dénoncés comme
Modérés s'affublèrent du Bonet rouge!
Les femmes rioient de voir leur mari si élégamant coëffés.*

51 'Les Tricoteuses ... (un) Jacobin ... Le Bonnet
Rouge', attributed to Pierre-Etienne Le Sueur.

The *tricoteuses*, paid-up supporters of Robespierre, and
of a ferocious reputation, wear the costume of the
respectable working class – a mob cap, a cotton or
woollen dress, plain apron and a printed kerchief.

While the ardent Jacobin argues for a motion at the
tribune, the more moderate citizen finds it prudent to
abandon his wig and three-cornered hat in favour of
the *bonnet rouge*.

83

REFRAINS PATRIOTIQUES

Si vous aimez la danse,
Venez accourez tous ,
Boire du Vin de France . (bis)
Et danser avec nous .

Dansons la carmagnole
Vive le son vive le son ,
Dansons la carmagnole
Vive le son du canon .

Ah ! ça ira ça ira ça ira ,
Le Peuple en ce jour sans cesse repete :
Ah ! ça ira ça ira ça ira ,
Réjouissons nous le bon temps viendra .

A Paris Rue du Théâtre Francais, N.º 4 .

52 'Refrains Patriotiques', 1792.

This engraving (accompanied by some verses from the popular revolutionary song *Ça Ira*) is an allegory showing the forces of reaction being routed by French patriotic ardour; working-class enthusiasts for the Revolution dance around a Liberty tree set up near the captured Bastille, while a *sans-culotte* points to a fleeing Austrian army. The women, notably tidier in their clothing than the men, wear the customary scarf knotted over a cap, a shoulder kerchief, jacket, skirt and apron. The men's clothes are patched and decrepit, two of them without even a shirt. The most revolutionary in dress, the *sans-culotte* with his *bonnet rouge* and ragged trousers, is the most martial in sentiment and accoutrements as he encourages the dancing of the carmagnole.

festivals which were inspired by the heroic virtues of republican Rome, but among their own club rituals one can see signs of the influence of Roman practices, such as the wearing of the *bonnet rouge*. At meetings of the Jacobins, where the decoration comprised such cult objects as the painted tricolour and the 'Eye of Surveillance', and the inscription 'Liberté, Egalité, Fraternité! ou la Mort', the president of each club would initiate proceedings by symbolically donning the red cap of liberty. This cap, according to the author of *De l'Origine et de la Forme du Bonnet de la Liberté* (1796), was worn not just when slaves in ancient Rome were given their freedom, but on all occasions of regained liberty from the yoke of tyranny;[7] red was also the colour of blood shed in the cause of the Revolution.[8]

As the most universally recognized badge of liberty, the red cap was also worn by the Cordeliers Club; Chateaubriand attended one of their meetings in 1792, and noted that on the president's table were red caps to be worn by speakers before they ascended the tribune.[9] The Cordeliers had been founded by Danton to give the *sans-culottes* an organized voice in politics, and the *bonnet rouge* was to become almost synonymous with this class from 1792.

The sight of a woollen bonnet rouge *fills the* sans-culotte *with joy, and let no one mock him for it. His enthusiasm is both praiseworthy and well founded. He has been told that in Greece and Rome this woollen cap was the symbol of freedom and the rallying sign for all those who hated despotism. With this in mind, his first desire is to become the owner of a* bonnet rouge.[10]

This cap of liberty had played a prominent part at the *Fête de la Fédération*, and the day after, in the ruins of the Bastille, someone planted a pike surmounted by such a cap.[11] The pike was a fearsome reminder of popular power; at the storming of the Tuileries on 10 August 1792 many of the *sans-culottes* carried pikes or bayonets on which were impaled 'rags of the clothes which

they had torn from the bodies of the dead Swiss'.[12] The somewhat anarchic tendencies of the *sans-culottes* could at times cause both fear and irritation among the Jacobins who preferred violence sanctioned by the force of law; an attempt to make the wearing of the *bonnet rouge* compulsory for all Jacobins in the spring of 1792 was successfully vetoed by Robespierre, who stated that the tricolour cockade was visible enough proof of patriotism.[13] In any case, the red bonnet appeared on many articles of everyday usage, such as pottery; it was painted on carriages, on milestones, inspired articles of jewellery,[14] and it was proposed in the journal *Annales Patriotiques* (1 August 1790) that the *bonnet rouge* replace the cock on church steeples and bell towers.

It is easier to define what the *sans-culottes* wore, than what they were, the vocal element of the working classes with, from the summer of 1792, hitherto unheard-of access to power at the highest level. After the invasion of the Tuileries on 10 August and the September massacres which followed, foreign visitors at least took rather a jaundiced view of what Dr Moore described as 'le Peuple Souverain'; 'these people dance about the streets, singing hymns to liberty, without regarding the despotism exercised in their sight, without reflecting that their fellow citizens are imprisoned every day nobody knows why, and that they themselves may be arrested to-morrow with as little reason'.[15] To such observers, France – a country long noted for its love of reason – had suddenly gone mad, and nowhere was the insanity more apparent than in the sudden emergence of the *sans-culottes*. Apart from the *bonnet rouge*, their costume was the typical working dress of the eighteenth century, and without particular significance except as a proud statement of class during the Revolution. Their name, according to Mercier, came from the word given to inelegantly dressed authors in the early eighteenth century,[16] but in the context of the Revolution, when *culottes* or knee-breeches were identified with the aristocracy, those without them could be seen to symbolize republicanism. Richard Twiss claimed that the *sans-culottes*' 'standard ... [is] an old pair of breeches, which they carry on the top of a pike, thrust through the waistband'; he noted, however, that 'these people have breeches, but this is the name that has been given to the mob'.[17]

Loose, baggy trousers (*le pantalon*), the sign of the worker in manual trades, were worn by large numbers of the *sans-culottes*, along with a short jacket (*le carmagnole*) and *sabots*, or wooden shoes, which helped to save leather for the soldiers' footwear at the front. The *carmagnole* was named after Carmagnola near Turin, the home of many of the originally Italian settlers in Marseilles; it also gave its name to a song and a dance. (It was the *fédérés* from Marseilles who in the summer of 1792 brought with them to Paris a new song written by Rouget de Lisle, which became the French national anthem.)

It goes without saying that personal adornments were frowned on, save for the tricolour cockade, or such items as metal brooches stamped with the head of Brutus or Marat, or pins and brooches in the form of *fasces* [18] (the bundle of rods which in ancient Rome symbolized unity and fraternity). Such political badges would be worn to indicate republican zeal, in the debating assemblies of the Paris *sections*, which had been composed to begin with of middle-class elements, but which by 1793 were in the hands of the *sans-culottes*, with some Jacobin support.[19]

The new government was determined to get as far away as possible from *ancien régime* manners and civility; they remembered perhaps the insults offered at first by courtiers in the Tuileries to the simply attired deputations from the Assembly visiting the king.[20] The rough costume of the working man became a badge of political virility and credibility. Along with the abandonment of polite address and the introduction of *tutoiement*, came a deliberate slovenliness in dress. Marat, for example, was described by Madame Tussaud as wearing a 'pepper and salt coat in the English

L'exclusif

53 'L'exclusif', from M. Beauvert's *Caricatures Politiques*, 1797–8.

This character symbolizes the extreme republican with ardently Jacobin views. He wears a greyish-brown *carmagnole* jacket with a red collar, matching woollen trousers buttoned up the side (a style worn for manual labour throughout the eighteenth century), and a black hat over dishevelled locks. The aggressive uncouthness of his appearance is enhanced by his wooden club, and the pipe which he never, (so we are told) takes out of his mouth.

fashion, with large lapels', top boots, a round hat and altogether 'a dingy neglected appearance, not very clean'.[21] Some of the more ferocious republicans were characterized by Beauvert in his *Caricatures Politiques* (published during the Directory when it was safe to attack the *sans-culottes*, but when the memory of their appearance and behaviour was still very vivid): 'Ce sont des patriotes vigoureux qui n'ont foi qu' à leur reliques, et qui ne peuvent se mettre dans la tête que l'égoisme, l'orgueil et l'ignorance . . . Ils sont pour la plupart d'une humeur inquiète, brusque et suspectante . . .' Such 'exclusifs' (see fig. 53), he says, wear dirty clothes, which consist of 'une veste courte et d'un gros pantalon de laine', shoes fastened with straps, and a shapeless hat; their hair is neglected, a pipe is constantly stuck in their mouth, and they carry a club to frighten off any opponents.[22] Noisily bellicose, the visible signs of their patriotism, commented Helen Maria Williams, 'were dirty linen, pantaloons, uncombed hair, red caps or black wigs'.[23] Although as a group they are difficult to pin down, they were often small shopkeepers, traders and craftsmen, inward-looking and chauvinistic (they could afford ostentatious patriotism as many were over military age). Soboul notes how the militant *sans-culotte* idealized the simplicity of his daily existence, and how he 'was born moralizer, quick to identify his own way of life with the practice of republican virtues'.[24]

Men had the opportunity for political debate and action; working-class women, on the other hand, who bore the brunt of carrying on the means of survival, and who were, on the whole, less politically motivated, were roused only by extraordinary circumstances to play a part in the Revolution. Michelet noted one such dramatic occurrence: 'Les hommes ont fait le 14 juillet, les femmes le 6 octobre. Les hommes ont pris la Bastille royale, et les femmes ont pris la royauté elle-même, l'ont mise aux mains de Paris, c'est-à-dire de la Révolution'.[25] The implication, that women had been quick to grasp the essentials of

54 'La Femme du Sans-Culotte', 1792.

Apart from the martial weapons (the sword carried, blade upwards, is probably looted from the Swiss guard at the storming of the Tuileries on 10 August), the costume is mainly that of a respectable working-class woman of the period – striped woollen (or linsey-woolsey) skirt, tight-fitting jacket, striped kerchief tucked into the apron bib, thick stockings and *sabots*. A more modish and revolutionary aspect to this costume is the cotton scarf head-dress trimmed with a cockade (this is a style taken up by the fashion magazines and described usually as *à la paysanne*); here it is worn over a frilled linen cap, the customary wear of working-class and middle-class women in the late eighteenth century.

FRANÇAISES DEVENUES LIBRES.

. . . . Et nous aussi, nous savons combattre et vaincre.
Nous savons manier d'autres armes que l'aiguille et le fuseau. O Bellone !
compagne de Mars, a ton exemple, toutes les femmes ne devroient-elles pas
marcher de front et d'un pas égal avec les hommes ? Déesse de la force et
du courage ! du moins tu n'auras point à rougir des *FRANÇAISES*.

Extrait d'une Lettre des Amazones à Bellone.

De la Collection Générale des Caricatures sur La Révolution Française de 1789.

Paris chez Villeneuve Graveur, rue Zacharie, St Séverin Maison du Perruquier Nº 21.

55 'Françaises devenues libres', 1789.

This engraving depicts the feminist leader Théroigne de Méricourt dressed for action, having broken the shackles which confined women to a passive role in society. The costume closest in style to a military uniform is a riding habit and boots; although the skirt is short, for greater ease of movement, the jacket has the high collar, tight sleeves and double-breasted fastening seen in fashion plates.

played a vigorous part in the early tumultuous events of the French Revolution, and in political debates (from the galleries) in the Paris *sections*. With defiant pride in the working–class garments of the time – the jacket (*carmagnole*), coarse woollen skirt, *sabots* and head-kerchief – such women as Dickens's Madame Defarge, glorying in the violence of the Revolution, certainly existed.

Trying to harness this new revolutionary force, and at the same time to fight for female participation in politics, were a number of feminist[26] leaders. Some were mavericks and acted as individuals rather than as part of a group. They included Théroigne de Méricourt, who had joined the women's march in October 1789, an ardent advocate of an armed female battalion, and whose customary attire was 'a blue riding habit, a cap of liberty on her head, and . . . a brace of pistols stuck in her girdle';[27] there was also the prolific writer Olympe de Gouges, who had argued for universal suffrage and equality with men – her famous phrase, 'La femme a le droit de monter à l'échafaud; elle doit avoir également le droit de monter à la tribune'[28] – sounded hollow in the ears of female activists when she was guillotined during the Terror.

The revolutionary government were worried as much about the appearance of these women, as about their political views, although the two were connected. Many of the women wore clothes that were either masculine in influence (like the riding habit of Théroigne de Méricourt) or in reality, like Claire Lacombe whose 'crimson trousers, red cap and tri-coloured scarf' were noted by John Gideon Millingen.[29] It has been noted that English riding habits, throughout the 1780s, were identified with egalitarian sympathies; the freedom of movement which they gave was additionally useful for the martial revolutionary woman. The wearing of masculine clothing struck at the deepest fears of men, imbued with the biblical notion that the sexes should be distinguished by their dress, and worried about

the revolutionary situation, by bringing the royal family back to Paris, was one not lost on either the women themselves or their (masculine) rulers. The latter had a real fear of the unleashed ferocity of the female *sans-culottes*, who had

Club Patriotique de Femmes.

Des Femmes bien Patriotes avoient formées un Club danslequel nétoit admise aucune autres;
Elles avoient leur Présidente et des sécrataires; on s'assembloit deux fois la semaine, la Présidente
faisoit la Lecture des Séances de la convention nationale, on approuvoit ou l'on critiquoit ses Decrets,
Ces Dames animées du zéle de la Bienfaisance faisoient entr'elles une collecte qui étoit distribuée à des
familles de bons Patriotes qui ont besoin de secours.

what usurpation of their authority this might portend.

With this in mind, and as part of their determination to stamp out feminist movements for universal suffrage, the republican government discouraged the wearing of the *bonnet rouge* by women; it was a belief firmly held by the Jacobins that once women wore such bonnets by right, they would demand more substantial political freedoms. This was one of the main complaints against the radical women's group, the

56 '*Club Patriotique de Femmes*', attributed to Pierre-Étienne Le Sueur.

The Revolution encouraged the setting-up of women's clubs to discuss political and social matters of particular relevance to their sex. Largely middle-class in composition, this is reflected in their clothing, neat gowns topped with large kerchiefs or shawls, and fashionable ribboned hats or bonnets.

Société des Républicaines-Révolutionnaires (SRR), led by Pauline Léon and Claire Lacombe, and in existence from February to October 1793. They were described as 'women, calling themselves Jacobines, from an allegedly revolutionary society ... in pantaloons and red bonnets ... [who] intended to force other citoyennes to wear the same costume'.[30]

Street disturbances between the proselytizing members of the SRR and the market women of Paris who did not wish to be converted to the

57 *Madame Lecerf*, 1794 François Gérard.

During 1794 a modest simplicity in dress is essential. Here, the artist's cousin wears a plain brown dress with drawstring neck, into which is tucked a white kerchief; a shawl covers her shoulders and what may be the short sleeves of her gown. The only touches of frivolity in her costume are a glimpse of coloured beads at her neck, and a white satin ribbon on the front of her cap, which has the obligatory cockade.

wearing of the red cap of liberty (they claimed that it was men's wear, and that being forced to wear it might lead to them having their hair cut and being sent to the front) caused the closing down of what has been described as 'the first political interest group for common women known in western history'.[31] Although it included some participation by *sans-culotte* women, such a society was bound to be dominated by the educated and articulate middle class; there were not enough of them however, to make much impact, and their programme of political, legal and educational equality for women was overshadowed by arguments about tactics, and lost sight of in quarrels about clothing. They were portrayed by the authorities as rabble-rousers; the sight of politically active women was distasteful to men reared on the doctrine of Rousseau that the feminine role was to be wife and mother, and to bring up her children imbued with republican virtues. In Robespierre's Republic of Virtue, inspired by Rousseau's ideas on morality, there was to be no place for an organized pressure group of women.

No doubt, during the Terror, it proved essential – especially in some of the more radical sections of Paris – to adopt the badges and slogans of *sans-culottisme*; equally, of course, many (possibly the majority) were fervent believers in the Revolution, without recourse to the brutality and vindictiveness which marked much of public life during 1793–4.[32] Revolutionary zeal was also intensified by conditions of particular hardship caused by bad harvests and rising prices, which led the National Convention to fix a maximum price on essential commodities, in September 1793; these included 'le lin, les laines, les étoffes, les toiles, les sabots'. These, it will be noticed, are everyday working-class fabrics, for luxury goods (as well as being politically and economically out of court for the poor) had almost disappeared. Many women had been put out of work by the decline in such industries as silk, lace and embroidery, all of which had been vital parts of the

58 *Fête à la Vieillesse*, 1794, Pierre-Alexandre Wille.

As part of the civic religion encouraged by the authorities of the new republic, this festival dedicated to Old Age is typical of the sort of celebrations (honouring such concepts as 'Youth', 'Agriculture' etc.) which were held all over France. Although the element of revolutionary propaganda is very evident – note the statue of Liberty, the central group of municipal officials in their tricolour sashes of office, and the young girls in flowered coronets and white gowns who vow only to marry 'jeunes républicains défenseurs de la patrie' – entertainment and merrymaking are the order of the day, following a long

French economy during the eighteenth century.[33] Then, as during the French Revolution, clothing was a highly prized commodity; before the advent of cheap cottons, men and women of the poorer classes had to rely on the second-hand trade, and the skill of the *revendeuse* at alterations.[34] Often, clothing had been handed down from one member of a family to another, as Richard Cobb notes in his perceptive and sympathetic study of some of the suicides in Paris

tradition of local fairs where enjoyment prevails over ideology.

during the Directory.[35] These men and women, at the lowest ebb of their fortunes, were still able to express individuality through clothing, to wear 'the harlequin colours of the very poor', to incorporate in their dress, for example, the bright colours of some recycled military uniform, polished buttons, and gay printed kerchiefs. Several layers of clothing were worn, both as portable wealth and for warmth, much of it carefully darned and mended. Cobb's study (as applicable, presumably, to the early years of the Revolution as to the Directory) brings the appearance of the poor into sharper focus; they exist as people, and not just as colourful extras in the genre scenes of the Revolution.

Yet even in the relatively static society described by Cobb, dress, as an expression of individuality and self-respect, must change with the times, and be subject to a greater or lesser extent to the rule of fashion. The informed opinion of Richard Twiss in the summer of 1792 was that 'the common people are in general much better clothed than they were before the Revolution'. He found women in 'white linen or muslin gowns' and large caps;[36] no tight lacing or high-heeled shoes were to be seen – not surprisingly, as these were the marks of ladies of rank, who, he says, stayed most of the time indoors. The men wore long greatcoats, and these *redingotes* (the most classless of male garments) turn up among the clothing of Cobb's suicides, along with the shirt, *gilet/veste*, *culottes* or trousers, i.e. the wardrobe of the working man. The formal coat, (*habit*), of the upper-class man, and the suit, the preserve of the professional man, are hardly to be seen.

On the premise that 'man does not live by bread alone' (even the very poor), and impelled by the need to substitute – in place of the Church – some sense of ritual and ceremony in life, the republican government instituted the religion of the state. From the very beginning of the Revolution the days of the Church had been numbered, with the nationalization of its property,

the suppression of religious orders, and the Civil Constitution of the Clergy in the summer of 1790. A decree of 6 April 1792 suppressed religious congregations, and prohibited (except on rare occasions) the wearing of ecclesiastical dress as inimical to equality. The religious credo of the approaching republic was as follows: 'Une nation libre ne doit révérer que deux choses: la loi et la vertu.'[37]

Patriotic virtue was expressed in trees of liberty, first planted in 1790; travelling between Calais and Paris in the summer of 1792, Richard Twiss found in every town such a tree, usually a poplar, decorated with the Cap of Liberty and tricolour ribbons.[38] *Autels de la Patrie* were also set up from 1790; a decree of 26 June 1792 stated that all *communes* had to set up such altars with the inscription, 'Le citoyen naît, vit et meurt pour la patrie'.[39]

A decree in the spring of 1794 established patriotic festivals to commemorate the great events of the Revolution, 14 July 1789, 10 August 1792, 21 January 1793 (the death of Louis XVI) and 31 May 1793 (the downfall of the Girondins); such *fêtes* (along with other festivals dedicated to more abstract concepts like youth, old age, industry, nature, and the martyrs of liberty), were meant to inculcate, according to Robespierre, 'des idées religieuses et morales avec les principes républicains'.[40] It was Robespierre, inspired by Rousseau, who decreed the establishment of the worship of the Supreme Being; churches were converted into Temples of Reason and on their façades was to be inscribed 'Le Peuple Français reconnaît l'existence de l'Etre Suprême et l'immortalité de l'âme'.[41] Christianity had been too closely identified with the old order, and now reason was to take the place of revelation.

However, a deity was still needed, appearing in the guise of a Goddess of Reason in white muslin robe and blue cloak (the imagery of the Madonna was still current); she sat on the throne of Liberty, with a red bonnet on her head, and holding a pike.[42] The pike itself might have been

59 'Fête de l'Être Suprême au Champ-de-Mars', 1794, Thomas-Charles Naudet.

This festival, although ostensibly to honour the new religion of the Supreme Being, was a celebration of the apotheosis of Robespierre. David's design included, on the right, the chariot of Ceres, goddess of harvests, but the focal point was a mountain crowned with a Tree of Liberty, and a vast statue of Hercules (who symbolized the French people). Watched by a large crowd, members of the Convention, led by Robespierre, climb to the top of the mountain.

made from the iron rails taken from churches; Twiss comments on this use of church property in the summer of 1792,when he notes that the statues of Christ and the saints were decorated with red caps and cockades.[43] Some months later, many churches were almost totally stripped of ornaments; if we are to believe Mercier in Le *Nouveau Paris*, chasubles hung side by side with pantaloons at the *fripiers* (dealers in second-hand clothes), 'terrorists' were dressed in *culottes* made from velvet vestments and shirts from choirboys' white albs, and groups of frenzied *sans-culottes*, draped in religious garments, danced the carmagnole.[44]

The apotheosis of Robespierre's power was the great *Fête de l'Etre Suprême* of 8 June 1794. An immense amphitheatre was erected in front of the centre pavilion of the Tuileries, before which were placed statues of Atheism, Discord and Egotism; after a quasi-religious service including a hymn to the Supreme Being, Robespierre set fire to the statues, and then headed a march to the Champ de Mars where a huge artificial mountain had been built. Robespierre led the members of the Convention, all dressed in blue coats with tricolour sash and plumed hat, to sit on the mountain; there were further hymns and salvos of artillery, and the people lifted up their children to consecrate them to the Supreme Being. Each Paris *section* elected favoured citizens to sit on the mountain;[45] matrons and young girls were dressed in white with a tricolour sash, children in white tunics crowned with violets, and men were either in the uniform of the National Guard, or in what various accounts describe as 'Roman' dress. The designer of this festival was David, and it was inevitable, given his academic training and the links that were constantly being made between the ancient world and the Revolution, that the imagery used should be classical. David had worked in Rome for some years, and he found classical allusions the perfect framework for his moral themes and republican ideals; classical themes, in any case, were part of the repertoire of an academic artistic tradition going back to the Renaissance. How far David's vision of antiquity led him to republicanism (or vice versa) is not clear; what we do know is that David, as official artist of the Revolution, aimed to demonstrate the nobility of the revolutionary cause by linking it to an admired classical past.

In this he was not alone, for there were many who thought they were living through times as full of heroic passions – courage, virtue, danger – as during the great days of the classical past; Helen Maria Williams, for example, writing in 1792, thought the French Revolution 'abounds with circumstances that would embellish the page of the Greek or Roman Annals . . . Succeeding generations will perhaps associate the Tenniscourt of Versailles and the Champ de Mars with the Forum and the Capitol . . .'[46] French society was imbued with knowledge of the classical past from an early age; H. T. Parker in *The Cult of Antiquity and the French Revolution* has demonstrated how the *collèges* of the *ancien régime* taught their pupils to admire the heroes and the literature of the great days of the Roman Republic. Madame Roland recalled how she wept at not having been born a Spartan or a Roman[47] and the actress Louise Fusil remembered: ''91 nous transforma en Spartiates et en Romains; tout nous

rappelait les temps antiques, les tableaux de David, les meubles des appartements, les costumes de Talma . . .'[48]

The influence of the classical past was everywhere. Six weeks after the fall of the Bastille, David exhibited at the Salon his *Lictors returning the bodies of his sons to Brutus*, which caught the mood of the summer of 1789; Brutus had destroyed a decadent monarchy, but found himself obliged to condemn to death his two sons who had conspired against the Roman Republic. The uncompromising moral of the subordination of family bonds to the demands of the state pointed the way to events under the Terror. Then it was Robespierre who carried his love of Sparta to extremes in his notion of sacrifice for the greater good for the state.[49]

After the outbreak of war, England was no longer looked on as the land of enlightenment, but one of the homes of reaction; France turned for comfort and parallels to the classical past. When, in the spring of 1793, the National Convention moved into the Tuileries, the decoration included statues of such noble heroes as Brutus and Cincinnatus, *fasces* and crowns of laurel were painted on imitation marble walls along with the stencilled red cap of liberty, and the President's chair was draped with silks *à la romaine*.[50] Classicism, especially in the work of its greatest exponent, David, was linked with Jacobinism; grand, noble and terrible ideals on a large scale were the order of the day, forcing the last vestiges of the old, self-indulgent, princely rococo art forms underground, whence they would re-emerge, during the Empire, as part of the cult of historical romanticism, *le style troubadour*.

The festivals designed by David and his team were among the greatest triumphs of propaganda during the French Revolution; they were intended to replace devotion to Church and King with loyalty to the nation and to the Revolution. One of the aims of propaganda is to inculcate a fierce patriotism, an emotion which was felt to be especially necessary when France was belea-

60 '*Triomphe de Voltaire*', 1791, engraved by Pierre Gabriel Berthault after Jean-Louis Prieur, from *Tableaux Historiques de la Révolution Française*, 1817.

The *Tableaux Historiques* set out in 1791 to be a definitive contemporary record of the great events of the Revolution. Here the artist (Prieur – an ardent revolutionary who was guillotined in 1795) depicts the elaborate cortège about to cross the Pont Royal, accompanied by members of the National Assembly, representatives of the municipality of Paris, the National Guard, the revolutionary clubs, and a number of foreign ambassadors. The funeral chariot is acompanied by 'les élèves des arts, habillés à l'antique' and is preceded by a statue of the seated Voltaire, carried by men in classical costume. J. G. Millingen noted that 'all the actors and actresses, singers and dancers of the different theatres were grouped round a statue of the philosopher in the various costumes of his *dramatis personae*'.

guered by internal and external foes. The *Journal de la Société Républicaine des Arts* (1794), the official organ of the Jacobin government, commented: 'Les fêtes Républicaines que nous célébrons sont un lien qui réunit les hommes . . . Les emblèmes, les trophées, la douce harmonie des instrumens, tout concourt à électriser les coeurs; c'est dans ces momens d'allégresse universelle que nous sommes grands et terribles à nos ennemis.'[51]

David's first full-scale pageant based on classical symbolism was the ceremonial procession taking the remains of Voltaire to the church of St Geneviève, renamed the Panthéon, on 11 July 1791. The cortège had as its centrepiece the funeral triumphal car which was drawn by twelve attendants in Roman costume; David's sketches of classical dress, with which he filled his notebooks when in Rome, proved a useful source. There were also twenty young girls dressed in white robes, led by Voltaire's adopted daughter crowned with laurels and holding a golden lyre.

Whatever the occasional absurdities of such festivals (and there were many to criticize them, both at the time – Madame de Genlis found the fête to Voltaire 'foolish, abominable and ridiculous' – and later when Carlyle damned them as 'so much unadulterated Mumbo-Jumbo'), they were a form of street theatre in which all could take part, and feel that the Revolution was a continuing process; they could be enjoyed on various levels even if some of the more abstruse allegorical and classical allusions escaped the crowd.

A member of the Jacobin club from early in 1790, and an outspoken enthusiast for the Revolution, David was a Paris deputy to the National Convention, and had voted for the death of the king. It was his firm belief that art must be used to advance the cause of the Revolution; it was obvious that festivals of the sort he designed (ten in all) could reach a wider audience than more traditional art forms, or the more conventional theatre. It has been pointed out that he must have

61 *La fête de l'unité, 10 Août 1793* (detail), Pierre-Antoine de Machy.

This festival, organized by David, celebrated the downfall of the monarchy and the first anniversary of the Republic. In the Place de la Révolution (formerly Place Louis XV) a plaster statue of Liberty was raised on the 'pedestal of tyranny', i.e. on the pedestal of the statue of Louis XV knocked down after the events of 10 August 1792. The emblems of monarchy are burnt in front of a crowd which includes members of the National Guard, *sans-culottes* and their womenfolk.

1 *Queen Marie-Antoinette with her children, 1785,* Adolf-Ulrik Wertmüller.

The setting is the English Garden of the Petit Trianon at Versailles. The Queen wears a *robe à la turque* of brown silk over white, trimmed at the hem with point net machine lace; her *fichu* and sleeve ruffles are of French needle lace. Her *pouf* of ribbons and feathers is probably by Rose Bertin. The little Dauphin wears a blue silk skeleton suit, in the English style, but with the badge and ribbon (the *cordon bleu*) of the order of the Saint-Esprit. His sister, Madame Royale, wears a muslin chemise which she lifts up to show the blue silk skirt underneath.

2 *Maximilien de Robespierre,* Louis-Léopold Boilly.

The fervent revolutionary and man of intense moral purpose, described by Thomas Carlyle as the 'seagreen Incorruptible', wears the clothes of a dandy of the *ancien régime;* shot-silk coat, nankeen breeches fastened with diamond buckles, buckled shoes and a powdered wig.

ie du Champ de Mars dit de la Federation à la Journeé mémorable du 14 Juillet 1790 au moment de l'arrivée de l'Assembleé Nationale
des Deputés de tous les Départements du Royaume et des Corps Militaire de Terre et de Mer

Autel de la Patrie 2 Le Trône du Roi 3. Loges pour les Membres de l'Assembleé Nationale et la Famille Royale 4 Place des Membres de la Municipalité et des Commissaires des Districts de Paris 5 l'Arc de Triomy
Passage de distance en distance pour la commodité de la circulation publique 7. Escaliers en dedans et en dehors pour éviter les embarras de la foule . 8. Batiments de l'Ecole Royale Militaire .
avoit placé dans tout le pourtour du Champ, trente rangées de Bancs pour asseoir 260000 spectateurs. Il restoit un espace derrière pour en contenir encor plus de 200000 ; debout .

3 *View of the Champ de Mars, 14 July 1790.*

The first anniversary of the fall of the Bastille was celebrated by a lavish spectacle on the
Champ de Mars. In the foreground National Guard *fédérés* can be seen marching through
a triumphal arch. In the centre Talleyrand celebrates mass at the Altar of the Nation,
and in the background, at the far end of the arena, is the King on a raised throne. The
enthusiasm of the participants and the spectators was not dampened by the weather,
the torrential rain indicated by the large number of umbrellas visible in the stands.

4 *Planting the Tree of Liberty,* attributed to Pierre-Etienne Le Sueur.

From the summer of 1790, Liberty trees were planted all over France to commemorate the Revolution. Here, the mayor (holding a shovel) and two municipal officers, backed up by National Guardsmen, watch the planting of such a tree carried out by a number of *sans-culottes,* two of whom wear the *bonnet rouge.* The tricolour is everywhere, from the cockades pinned to hats, to the sashes worn by the mayor and his colleagues, and by the three female singers dressed in the simple white cotton gowns which became *de rigueur* for women taking part in the great revolutionary festivals of the early 1790s.

5 *Portrait of a woman, c. 1794–5*, attributed to the circle of David.

The sitter, sometimes identified as Thérèse Tallien, is attired in the costume of a fashionable *demi-mondaine*, a revealing and expensive simplicity. The classical past inspires the sleeveless cotton shift knotted on the shoulder, and the stole of fine yellow wool bordered with a Grecian design of interlinking black rings.

6 *M. Pierre Sériziat, 1795*, Jacques-Louis David.

David's portrait of his wife's brother-in-law was painted in the country after the artist was released from prison in October 1795. But for the revolutionary cockade in his hat, Sériziat is dressed in the style of a fashionable English country gentleman, in a grey high-collared coat, chamois leather breeches, and top boots. With whip in one hand, and kid gloves in the other, he is seated on a green woollen riding cloak trimmed with gold braid.

Membre du Directoire Executif
dans son grand Costume.

7 *Membre du Directoire Exécutif dans son grand costume, 1795,*
Jacques Grasset de Saint-Sauveur.

The Directors' costume for formal occasions consists of a blue silk coat (*habit-manteau*) worn
over a white tunic and pantaloons. Gold embroidery trims the coat, the tunic, and the red
cloak, and the *tout ensemble* is completed by a black hat ornamented with a tricolour panache.

Cheveluro en porc-épic. Schall à Mouches. Rubans en Cothurn.

Dess. d'ap. Nat. sur le Boulevart des Capucines.

8 *Fashion plate* from the *Journal des Dames et des Modes, 14 Ventôse An VI* (4 March 1798).

Taken from life, we are told, as seen on the boulevard des Capuchines, the costume of this fashionable *élégante* consists of a spotted shawl edged in black velvet, and long-sleeved round robe, the skirts lifted *à l'antique* to display ankle ribbons in the style of classical *cothurnes*. The very short haircut (known as the *chevelure à la Titus*) is the invention of M. Duplan, 'un caprice fantasque ... qui n'a d'autre mérite que celui d'être à la mode'.

been familiar with Rousseau's *Lettre à d'Alembert sur les spectacles* (1758) in which the philosopher praised the festivals of antiquity, believing they were necessary to ensure the maintenance of law and order.[52] This was certainly prophetic, for during the Terror such festivals served as a kind of theatrical catharsis, a way in which the emotions of the people could be channelled into worship of the state; at this period it was essential to be seen attending such pageants, for any other

entertainment (except for the patriotic theatre) was thought too frivolous.

To commemorate the Massacre of the Champ de Mars (17 July 1791), David designed a great festival held on 15 April 1792. There was a huge triumphal car with a statue of Liberty on it, which, accompanied by a huge crowd including members of the radical clubs, left the faubourg St Antoine for the Bastille where the statue was dedicated, and then proceeded on to the Champ de Mars where a ritual purification took place.[53] Another vast statue – this time of the goddess of Nature – was built for the *Fête de la Réunion* of 10 August 1793; the theme being unity and indivisibility, the statue jetted out from her breasts the waters of regeneration, which were drunk by representatives of all the regions. The people marched in procession to the Champ de Mars, some holding banners which showed the all-seeing Eye of Surveillance; the procession, and accompanying set-pieces, took sixteen hours to enact. With the kind of organized belligerence, violent propaganda, and somewhat fake enthusiasm for peace which characterizes May-Day processions in Moscow, the people, some wearing the red cap of liberty, and others carrying olive branches and garlands of flowers, accompanied a

---

62 *Le Triomphe du Peuple*, Jacques-Louis David.

Perhaps a design for the theatrical production, '*La Réunion du Dix-Août, ou l'Inauguration de la République*', performed at the Opéra in April 1794, David depicts the triumph of the French people over the monarchy.

Victory flies in front of a chariot on which is seated Hercules with his club; he represents the French people and is accompanied by Equality and Liberty with their attributes, which include a cap of liberty on a pole. The chariot is preceded by citizens who crush the emblems of monarchy, and it rolls over the attributes of Despotism and Superstition. It is hailed, on the right, by martyrs of liberty, such as Brutus, William Tell, and Marat.

rudimentary hearse on which lay emblems of royalty.[54] This particular fête, which also commemorated the downfall of the monarchy on 10 August 1792, inspired a theatrical version, entitled 'La Réunion du Dix-Août, ou l'Inauguration de la République', performed in April 1794. It was one of the many dramatizations of contemporary events which increasingly took the place of the real theatre which was subject to censorship.[55] After the downfall of the monarchy, plays were 'revised' for republican ears, and any mention of royalty or aristocracy removed. 'Les costumes n'échappèrent pas à cette folie égalitaire, et la cocarde devint l'attribut indispensable de tout acteur'; cockades were placed on Minerva's helmet and Andromaque's robe, and many of the actresses appeared in white gowns decorated with tricolour sashes.[56]

The link between the Revolution and the theatre was often intimate. It was often an actress who took the role of the Goddess of Reason in the temples dedicated to the worship of the Supreme Being, and members of theatrical companies were involved in the republican festivals. David designed the costumes worn by his friend, the actor Talma (whose political views coincided with his own), in plays with classical themes, which were, of course, very popular. David's own well-known paintings and his drawings inspired classical costumes with a certain amount of historical accuracy[57] for the men who took part in the fêtes; for the women, white gowns in a neo-classical style were already fashionable, and needed very little addition to make them 'antique'. White dresses had been worn in fashionable and artistic circles during the 1780s (we recollect the famous *souper grec* organized by Vigée Le Brun in 1788 when her guests were clothed in white draperies, she herself wearing her usual 'white dress like a tunic'[58]), and they came into their own during the Revolution.

On 7 September 1789 the wives and daughters of a number of leading artists (Madame David among them), dressed in white and with tricolour cockades in their hair, publicly donated their jewellery to the National Assembly; the idea of such a gift to the state in need was inspired by a Roman story in Plutarch's *Parallel Lives*, a source familiar to educated men and women.[59]

White, with its connotations of the classical, of purity and sacrifice (Madame Roland and Lucile Desmoulins wore white gowns when they were guillotined, as did many others in an ironic echo of the republican ideal of martyrdom) was chosen by David for the gowns worn by women and girls at his festivals;[60] such a costume, decorated with a tricolour sash, combined the antique with the patriotic and the fashionable, and it is worth speculating how far David helped to make the white chemise gown the most important mode of the 1790s.

A more important concern of the artist was to stamp his views on the whole artistic scene, in pursuit of the glorification of the Republic. In Louis-Sébastien Mercier's prophetic *L'An 2440* (1770) the theatre has become a place where moral truths are disseminated, and in the Salon of the future there are only allowed to be works of art capable of inspiring virtue and the sublime; the aim of David was to depict, in painting, the most noble of heroic and civic virtues.

It is not surprising that, in the circumstances of the late eighteenth century, many of the greatest works of art are works of propaganda. Mozart's *The Magic Flute* (1791) is an expression of the ideology of 1789; via the ideas of the *philosophes*, the ideal society is inspired by Nature, Reason and Wisdom. An infinitely more chilling form of propaganda is David's great *Death of Marat*, (1793) where the assassinated revolutionary leader and journalist is depicted as a martyr of the people; this icon hung on one side of the President's chair in the National Convention.[61]

Many of David's energies during the turbulent years of Jacobin rule were, however, devoted to politics; he had his duties as a deputy and he was also a member of the Committee of General Security. He was also the guiding spirit behind

Des Citoyennes de Paris, Epouses d'Artistes, et de Marchands.
font hommage de leurs Bijoux à la convention Nationnale.

63 '*Des Citoyennes de Paris, Epouses d'Artistes, et de Marchands font hommage de leurs Bijoux à la convention Nationnale*', attributed to Pierre-Etienne Le Sueur.

Dressed in white and with tricolour sashes, these public-spirited citizenesses donate their jewellery to the government. From the early days of the Revolution, men and women were encouraged to give their valuables in this way to support the cause.

the organization of the arts, replacing the *ancien régime* academies with a *Commune des Arts* in 1790, which was itself abolished in favour of the *Société Populaire et Républicaine des Arts* in the autumn of 1793.[62] One of the functions of this society was to promote republican works of art;

among their wide-ranging interests was dress, and a number of artists, including David, were in the spring of 1794 given the brief of designing 'republican' costumes.

David's interest in costume was well known. Not only did he take the trouble to research the clothing of his great history paintings, but a similar enthusiasm informed the dress of the main protagonists in his republican festivals. These events were so reliant on David's skill and imagination that they virtually ended after the death of Robespierre in July 1794;[63] David was imprisoned and barely escaped with his life. In a sense he was the victim of his own success, for the last great revolutionary festival, the *Fête de l'Etre Suprême*, contributed to the downfall of Robespierre, when it was rumoured that he wished to impose a personal theocracy, and that he himself

99

Costume du françois Républiquain

64 'Costume du François Républiquain', c. 1794–5, Jean-Michel Moreau.

Moreau was a devoted republican, and this drawing may be the result of the revolutionary government's demand that artists submit designs for a national costume.

Apart from the loose jacket with wide revers and slits in the sleeve (the style may be inspired by contemporary theatrical costume à la François I), the outfit is more akin to actual fashion than the designs proposed by David. The hat is the fashionable round hat (although here trimmed with a feather); the waistcoat with prominent lapels is the style of the mid 1790s, as are the pantaloons which reveal the shape of the limbs like a classical nude.

was the Supreme Being to whom the French were asked to dedicate themselves.

All this was some time in the future, when David made his first recorded attempts at designing a costume for his fellow-citizens in 1792. Dr Moore's comments are worth quoting in full:

David, the celebrated painter, who is a Member of the Convention and a zealous Republican, has sketched some designs for a republican dress, which he seems eager to have introduced; it resembles the old Spanish dress, consisting of a jacket with tight trowsers, a coat without sleeves above the jacket, a short cloak which may either hang loose from the left shoulder or be drawn over both; a belt to which two pistols and a sword may be attached, a round hat and a feather are part of this dress, according to the sketches of David, in which full as much attention is paid to picturesque effect as to conveniency. This artist is using all his influence, I understand, to engage his friends to adopt it, and is in hopes that the Municipality of Paris will appear in it at a public feast or rejoicing . . . Part of this dress is already adopted by many, but I have only seen one person in public equipped with the whole, and as he had managed it, his appearance was rather fantastical. His jacket and trowsers were blue; his coat,

through which the blue sleeves appeared, was white with a scarlet cape; his round hat was amply supplied with plumage; he had two pistols stuck in his belt, and a very formidable sabre at his side; he is a tall man, and of a very warlike figure; I took him for a Major of Dragoons at least; on enquiring I find he is a miniature painter.[64]

Quite what this costume looked like is not clear; at this stage (especially with the 'Spanish' element, that is, the coat with slashed sleeves, and the short cloak hanging from one shoulder). it does not resemble the more classical designs which David was to produce in 1794. Which part of the costume was 'already adopted by many' is also rather confusing; possibly Moore means the 'tight trowsers' or pantaloons which were more common in France than in England. It seems likely that this early experiment with costume design was more a product of David's theatrical imagination than any serious equation of dress with republican ideals.

From the beginning of the Revolution, however, much consideration was given to the question of dress and how far appearances should contribute to the concept of equality. One of the first acts of the new National Assembly in October 1789 was to reject the official costumes which had been imposed on the Estates by court order and which, seem in fact to have been more honoured in the breach than in the observance. At first, with a sense of freedom from restraint, every deputy was allowed to wear what he liked, although peer custom and the virtual identification of democracy with a certain kind of informality, led to almost a uniform in men's dress. In October 1793 (8 Brumaire An II), Fabre-d'Eglantine successfully urged on the Convention the notion that citizens should be entitled to wear what costume they liked.

By this time, however, freedom had begun to give way to increasing sartorial censorship. It was a natural progression from the abolition of the noble order of the St Esprit in 1791,[65] to the notion that army officers should not wear distinguishing uniforms; 'If we are all equal ... we must put an end to the aristocracy of dress, particularly in the army,' was the comment made by Hébert in his violently revolutionary magazine, *Le Père Duchesne*.[66] The mainly *sans-culotte* readership of this journal were only too happy to enforce, with violence if necessary, the wearing of the cockade, made compulsory for men from July 1792.[67] Although from the spring of 1792 there was some discussion about the need for public officials to adopt some external marks of authority, it was the costume of the private citizen which began to attract attention.

During March 1794 the *Société Populaire et Républicaine des Arts* began to discuss what form such a costume might take; how could it suit both the countryman and the citizen in the town? How could it encompass some military element as an indication that men should all be ready to take up arms for the republic? How could it comply with Rousseau's vague dictum that dress should be useful and not luxurious, and yet be elegant and tasteful in design? These deliberations resulted in a pamphlet entitled *Considérations sur les avantages de changer le costume français*, published in April 1794, although no firm conclusions were reached except to state the need for a true republican costume appropriate to the principles of freedom.[68]

That such a costume was necessary, no-one seems to have doubted, in their eagerness to distance themselves both from the over-refined dress of the *ancien régime* and the unattractive clothing of the *sans-culottes*. A certain Amaury Duval, for example, a civil servant in the Arts and Sciences Bureau of the Ministry of the Interior, in the summer of 1794, attacked the mincing steps and exaggerated costume of the *muscadins* with their very short waistcoats, tight culottes and 'un frac d'une forme bizarre'; he also spoke out against the 'prétendus sans-culottes' with their short jackets and pantaloons. His solution to the costume problem was an outfit consisting of tunic and shorts, with a mantle. For women, he proposed a tunic; antique buskins were to replace stockings and shoes.[69]

Reactions to the views of the *Société Populaire et Républicaine des Arts* included two responses from women on their dress; one 'Césarine Boissard, amie de la nature' demanded the abolition of boned stays, and the other, 'une autre citoyenne, mère de famille, demanda le costume dans le genre antique'.[70] It would be tempting to think that women were too sensible to become involved in the somewhat absurd notion of dress reform, but, as their costume was already, in some forms, closer to classical styles, no great change was necessary. In addition, most men felt that women, being disenfranchised, were unworthy of true republican costume.

It was inevitable that when artists were invited to submit their designs (the hope was expressed that there would be 'un génie sublime qui produira le meilleur costume'),[71] David would be the choice, as the artist most associated with the Revolution. By a decree of 25 Floréal, An II (14 May 1794) he was asked to produce designs for civilian costume suitable 'aux moeurs républicaines. Et au caractère de la Révolution';[72] a further decree of 5 Prairial (24 May) stated that he should also submit designs for the legislature and for government officials. Eight designs by David survive; two are for civilian costumes, five official (including two for the representatives of the people), and one is a military habit.[73] This last (known only through an engraving) is similar to the costume designed by David for the *Elèves de Mars*, the republican military academy founded by Robespierre. Their uniform was described by Millingen as 'a brown frock coat or tunic, double-breasted, red trousers, and an elegant leather helmet; they wore no stiff stocks, but their shirt collars were broad and turned down. Their arms consisted of a musket, and a Roman sword of the most chaste design'.[74]

David's designs generally are a curious mixture of the classical, the historical and his own

65 *Costume designs*, 1794, Jacques-Louis David.

David's design on the left for the citizen depicts a tight-fitting frogged tunic and 'classical' tights. While the costume is ostensibly 'historical', it is imbued with the sartorial aesthetic of the mid 1790s, which emphasizes the shape of the body, while the cloak with its tasselled fastening looks forward to the styles of the early nineteenth century. On the right, David envisages the French deputies wearing a tunic similar to that worn by the citizen; tights, 'Roman' buskins, and a cloak fastening on the shoulder *à l'antique*. The citizen has a tricolour sash, and the *représentant du peuple* has a kind of tricolour cloak—blue with a red and white border. Both men are given feathered *toques* trimmed with a cockade.

artistic imagination; they are also inspired by theatre costume of the time. The tunics (long or short) and the open-sided mantles are influenced by the costume of classical antiquity, as are the swords and the plumed *toques*; however, as bare legs *à la romaine* could not be accepted by men long used to knee breeches or pantaloons, those wearing short tunics were to wear tights which the artist hoped would produce a passable imitation of antique nudity. These tunics, however, in their design and decoration, occasionally recall the costume of the sixteenth century, a form of theatrical shorthand for the dress of the historic past with which David would have been familiar.

It is not possible to know if David had read Louis-Sébastien Mercier's futurist fantasy, *L'An 2440 Rêve s'il en Fut Jamais* (*The Year 2440, a Dream of What Will Never Be*), which was published in 1770, and which in its description of the ideal dress of the future, anticipates many of the ideas discussed by the dress reformers of the French Revolution. When the narrator of this tale wakes up in the Paris of 2440 (a transformed capital with gracious squares, straight streets and a 'temple to Clemency' on the site of the destroyed Bastille), one of his first acts is to dress himself in the costume he sees all around him, a loose-fitting tunic fastening with a sash, tights and buskins, and over all a gown with wide sleeves;[75] the similarities to David's designs are quite striking.

Although the Committee of Public Safety instructed David to have thousands of his designs engraved[76] and those for civilian costume to be distributed around the country where it was hoped they would be adopted by leading citizens, the project was a failure. Dress reform, as Utopian dreamers and reformers before and since have found, cannot be achieved at the stroke of a pen; dress is one of the art forms most resistant to dogma and ideology, and it has its own rules, following on naturally from existing styles, as ceremonial and official dress originally evolved from high fashion.

The poet and playwright Antoine Arnault, while admiring the elegance of David's designs, and the perseverance of Talma in wearing such a costume although he was often taken for a foreign spy, admitted that the idea was not a success.[77] David's designs, as well as being considered risible by the average citizen weary of endless government directives, seem to have been adopted only by a few of the artist's friends and pupils; in any case, only a few weeks after the promulgation of the decrees on dress, the Jacobin regime was overthrown. The idea of a national dress for civilians was abandoned, although it appears that some of David's pupils – to his embarrassment – continued the cult of the antique during the Directory, and 'ran about the streets as real sans-culottes, with a short tunic, and a mantle or rather an ample toga . . .'[78]

Although the idea of a 'republican' civilian dress had proved unfeasible, the authorities continued to believe that some form of official costume was necessary to demonstrate the dignity of the revolutionary cause in the face of a largely hostile world. The Committee of Public Instruction, which had been set up by the *Société Populaire et Républicaine des Arts*, to inform people of the proper function of art in a republic, commissioned designs for a set of official costumes from Jacques Grasset de Saint-Sauveur; these were published under the title *Costumes des Représentans du Peuple Français* in 1795. This work was, according to the abbé Grégoire, 'le résultat des observations de plusieurs artistes distingués'.[79] David (under arrest until the revolutionary detainees were amnestied in late October 1795) was probably not included, but Grasset de Saint-Sauveur's designs, in their mixture of the classical and the historical, owe an obvious debt to the great artist. Instead of the Spartan theme beloved of the radical Jacobins, there is a new emphasis on luxury; 'Quel luxe, quel magnificence, quelle dignité dans le costume des Grecs, dans celui des Romains.' Such a costume could demonstrate both 'la fierté républicaine', and 'la richesse d'une

COSTUMES DES REPRÉSENTANS
DU PEUPLE FRANÇAIS

Membres des deux Conseils,
Du Directoire Exécutif, des Ministres,
Des Tribunaux, des Messagers d'Etat,
Huissiers, et autres fonctionnaires Publics

66 Frontispiece, *Costumes des Représentans du Peuple Français*, 1795, Jacques Grasset de Saint-Sauveur.

The state messenger, dressed in his official costume of tunic, tights and short cloak *à la Henri IV*, stands before the Council of Five Hundred in their long white robes, open-sided red cloaks, and velvet *toques*.

white double-breasted tunic also embroidered in gold, white silk pantaloons, tied around the waist by a blue silk sash with gold tassels, and a round hat with tricolour panache. On formal occasions the *grand costume* was similar in style, although the coat was blue, and there was a red silk cloak embroidered in gold.

To an unsympathetic observer like the duchesse d'Abrantès, the effect was often absurd: 'The Directory exhibited itself in all its burlesque pomp of mantles and hats with feathers which rendered the meeting of the five members of the supreme power sufficiently ridiculous.'[81]

The legislative body (comprising the *Council of Five Hundred* who initiated measures, and the *Council of Ancients* who either accepted or rejected them) were given long robes and mantles – a reminder that in ancient Rome dignity was equated with ample draperies. Such a costume was cumbersome and attracted criticism: 'au lieu de vouloir vêtir en Romains ou en prêtres les représentants du peuple français, il faut se rapprocher de nos usages'.[82]

In order, therefore, to make the legislators' costume closer in style to contemporary dress, and at the same time to keep something of the antique flavour, the representatives of the people by a decree of 29 Brumaire An VI (19 November 1797) were ordered to wear a blue coat with a gold-fringed tricolour sash at the waist, a red mantle *à la grecque* fastening on the shoulder, and a *toque* with a tricolour aigrette.

The concept of a distinctive legislative costume continued after the collapse of the Directory late in 1799. When curious English visitors during the short-lived Peace of Amiens (March 1802–May 1803) ventured across the Channel, many commented on the colourful costumes worn by the legislators of the Consulate. Most accounts were censorious – 'blackguards in masquerade' was a typical derisory comment – but at least one traveller found that the relative uniformity of attire 'presents a more imposing spectacle' than the 'variegated' clothing worn by

nation opulente';[80] the new Directory, while wishing to distance itself from the excesses of the Jacobin regime and at the same time honouring the ideals of republicanism, nevertheless believed that lavish official costumes would add lustre to the new government, and to France.

The most elaborate costume was worn by the five Directors, who acted as the executive power. This costume consisted of a short open coat (*habit-manteau*) of red embroidered in gold, a

67 *Fan depicting the official costumes of 1795.*

The costumes depicted (fifteen in all) range from the plumed splendour of the Directors in the centre, the 'classical' garb of the judges (on the left), the Five Hundred and the Ancients, and the sober, dark costumes of government officials and administrators. On the far right is the mayor with his tricolour sash.

notion that rich and splendid official costume (in a style which set it apart from everyday fashions) could be seen to represent the power and glory of France. The idea of such costumes, reinforcing the authority of a ruling élite and first dreamt up by the revolutionaries with the help of artists like David, was to be extended on a much wider scale when, under Napoleon, a court became the necessary corollary to the establishment of Empire in 1804.[84]

MPs in the House of Commons in London.[83]

While Napoleon may have occasionally found it irksome to wear the somewhat Ruritanian costume decreed for the Consuls, he accepted the

68 *'Député au Conseil des cinq cent 1797'*, c. 1797–8, engraved by François Séraphin Delpech after Alexis Chataignier.

Apart from the cloak and the feathered *toque*, the costume is closer in style to contemporary fashion than the antique official dress promoted during 1794–5, which was abandoned in 1797.

A mantle like the one depicted here survives in the Musée de la Mode et du Costume de la Ville de Paris; belonging either to the costume of the Ancients or the Five Hundred, it is of red casimir with blue wool embroidery.

4 | Decline and Fall: Thermidor and Directory 1794–1799

The period between the downfall of the Jacobin regime and the establishment of the Consulate has proved a puzzle to historians, some seeing it as a betrayal of the ideals of the Revolution, others seeing it as a prelude to the glorious assumption of power by Napoleon.

After the downfall of Robespierre and his supporters in July 1794, the Convention struggled to hammer out a new constitution which would avoid the horrors of dictatorship. This they had to do against a constant background of war, in which the fortunes of France ebbed and flowed, and continuing internal insurrection which was encouraged by the *émigrés*, and by hostile foreign powers.

The immediate aftermath of 9 Thermidor was a not-unexpected shift in power towards the centre and the moderates. In Paris the radical *commune* was disbanded (many of its members were guillotined), and late in 1794 the Jacobin clubs were closed down. In December the Girondins were recalled to government. It was a period of confusion and shifting political allegiances, of revenge being plotted and old scores being paid off; the Thermidorean reaction was most violent in the areas where the Terror had been most savage, and in the south in particular, there was a White Terror against the Jacobins. The extreme left was still a power to be reckoned with as it could support popular insurrections against the government, such as the bread riots of Germinal and Prairial (the winter of 1794–5 had been one of the harshest on record) which were exacerbated by the abolition of price controls. Fearful of a revival of *sans-culottisme*, the Convention ruthlessly suppressed the unrest.

The deliberations of the politicans produced a new constitution in October 1795, a bourgeois republic based on property owners; male adult suffrage was abandoned and active citizenship was limited to those who paid taxes on land or on personal property. The executive power was a directorate of five, and the legislative body comprised the Council of Five Hundred who proposed resolutions, and the Council of Ancients (they had to be aged over forty, and to be married or widowers) who examined them. It was a system doomed to political instability; over-zealous in their avoidance of a presidential form of government, they decided that every year one of the Directors had to resign, and one-third of the legislature. This was bound to lead to political in-fighting as the various factions and their supporters manoeuvred for power.

It is tempting, however, for the historian to pronounce with the virtue of hindsight. At the time, there was a genuine belief that the new constitution would provide a stable and reasonably liberal form of government which would preserve the gains of the Revolution and avoid a repetition of the Terror. As a symbol of the harmony which it was hoped would prevail, in October 1795 the Place de la Révolution, once the main site of the dreaded guillotine, was renamed the Place de la Concorde.

Caution and compromise had to guide the actions of government in the uncertain times following on the execution of Robespierre. There was, for example, dissension between those who returned to the Church (there was a revival, from 1795, of popular Catholicism, largely led by women), and those who adhered to the secular, republican calendar; the authorities had to steer carefully between the claims of *Monsieur Dimanche* and *Citoyen Décadi*, and both days became holidays by default. The restoration

L'ANARCHISTE

69 'L'Anarchiste', 1797.

The divided loyalties of many men under the Directory are made very clear. The seated central figure is half-dressed as a *sans-culotte* in short *carmagnole*, trousers and *sabots*, and half as an elegant man of fashion, in the *Incroyable* style, with tight-fitting coat and calf-length knee-breeches. One head looks towards the left, to grasp the hand of a working-class woman, a *tricoteuse*, with her coarse gown and kerchief. One head gazes, on the right, at a member of the *jeunesse dorée* dressed in the height of fashion.

The implication of the caption is that, in spite of the claims of both left and right, many men opt for neither extreme, and choose to go their own way.

70 *Portrait of a man, c.* 1795, Jean-Baptiste Wicar.

Wicar was a pupil of David, and a member of the *Société Populaire et Républicaine des Arts*; as such he took part in the discussions in the spring of 1794 on the subject of promoting a national, 'republican' dress.

Without doubt this is a portrait, intimate and sympathetic, of a friend with similar political beliefs. Dressed in the high-collared coat in the English style, *de rigueur* for the thinking republican, his dishevelled hair indicates perhaps an indifference – feigned or real – to fashionable elegance.

of freedom of worship early in 1795 allowed for the practice both of various republican religious cults (though not that of the Supreme Being), and of the traditional forms of Christianity. By the early years of the Consulate, however, Chris-

tianity had triumphed over 'civic religion based on the dogmas of Deism and the social values of Republicanism', and nearly all churches were restored to Christian worship.[1] Although the republican festivals continued after the fall of Robespierre[2] (a *fête du 9 Thermidor* was popular for a time), they aroused little enthusiasm among a populace which associated them with the agit-prop of a discredited regime. In addition, they ran the risk of causing public disorder, which the authorities feared; on one occasion in 1795, during the fête celebrating the death of Louis XVI (21 January), some young men of counter-revolutionary inclinations gathered in the gardens of the Palais-Egalité and set fire to a doll made in the image of Marat and clothed in Jacobin dress.[3] By the time of the Consulate, although 18 Brumaire (Napoleon's assumption of power) was celebrated with military parades, the only festival enthusiastically honoured by the people, in which they could be participants and not merely spectators, was that of 14 July, Bastille Day.

This was the one day, perhaps, when the French people could at least demonstrate a sense of unity and pay a tribute to the most noble of the ideals of the French Revolution, even if they had suffered as a result of the more extreme beliefs of some of its adherents. Many moderate republicans, like Mercier, found the Revolution a mixed blessing. It had been right to fight for freedom and against tyranny, but many brave citizens had been deceived by the demagogues of the Jacobin party; no-one setting out on the road towards liberty could have foreseen the terrible events of the Terror which had cost so many lives.

It was in a mood of considerable disillusionment, even cynicism, that Mercier sat down to record, in *Le Nouveau Paris* (1798), how much manners and dress had changed since before the Revolution. Some of the undoubted excesses of society (which he deplores) were due to a sense of relaxation and relief from the intolerable strain of Robespierre's Republic of Virtue. It is hardly

71 *'Le Petit Coblentz'*, c. 1797, Jean-Baptiste Isabey.

This is a satire on the *jeunesse dorée* promenading along the boulevard des Italiens, known as 'le petit Coblentz' due to its popularity with those in the fashionable world whose hearts were with the *émigrés* in the German Rhine town of Koblenz.

However, among the ultra-fashionable *beau monde* – the artist exaggerates the high cravats, tight coats, long and carefully bedraggled hair, and the mincing gait of the *Incroyables* – can be seen such undoubted supporters of the Revolution as Bonaparte and Talleyrand on the far right, behind the elongated figure of Madame Récamier on the arm of the royalist actor and singer, Pierre-Jean Garat.

surprising considering the years of privation and subterfuge – ('J'ai vécu,' said Sieyès when asked what he had done during the Terror), that when the need for discretion in all walks of life was over, men and women took full advantage of the freedom offered to them. The Directory's reputation for decadence and corruption has been somewhat exaggerated; it rests, perhaps, partly on the intensified enjoyment of the pleasures of life, achieved by a new, ambitious and rather raffish group of people who had often made their fortunes in rather dubious ways. It was a society in the process of being formed, full of rough edges to begin with, but in a few years considerably refined; when the diplomat Miot de Melito returned to Paris in 1798, after an absence of three years, he found that 'the too simple manners (and) the coarse language of the Republic under the Convention' had given way to a 'politeness of speech and elegance in manners and dress'.[4]

Each of the five Directors held court at the Luxembourg palace, the richest being that of Barras, who liked to imitate the style of the *ancien régime* and whose salon was presided over by the *demi-mondaine* Madame Tallien. Such women formed the new aristocracy, along with military men (the army, especially after the immensely successful first Italian campaign of Napoleon in 1796–7 was seen to be the way to fortune, both political and financial), army contractors and speculators; some *émigrés* began to trickle back, adding a veneer of courtly etiquette to social gatherings. Miot de Melito described the salons of the Directory as crowded with 'Contractors and Generals, with women of easy virtue, and ladies of the ancient nobility, with patriots and returned *émigrés*'.[5]

It was no longer necessary to hide wealth, but to enjoy spending it. Elegant town houses were built; the social centre of Paris shifted to the Right Bank, to the newly developing Chaussée d'Antin (where from 1798 Madame Récamier had her salon), and the area around the rue de Clichy. New pleasure gardens appeared; the Palais-Egalité, popular before the Revolution, had become too dissolute[6] and people of fashion preferred Tivoli and Frascati. The public gardens, however, were open to all, and all kinds of people were to be seen there. One fashionable journal describes there, among the modestly dressed married couples and the old who had lost all their money during the Revolution, an abbé who looked like a Jacobin, and rich women with more money than taste; one woman, living in a hovel four years ago, now apes the manners of the *demi-mondaine* leaders of fashion, with her carriage, her jewels and her cosmetics (she even changes her shoes for the the modish neo-classical sandals or *cothurnes*) but underneath, 'il lui reste

Élégante en Costume de Bal, les Cheveux relevés à la Grecque, à l'instant du repos après le Tournoiement d'une Valse.

72 *Fashion plate*, 1798, from the *Journal des Dames et des Modes*.

A fashionable couple dance the waltz. The man wears a green coat with a high collar, buff knee-breeches, white stockings and black pumps. His partner's costume, according to the editor of the *Journal*, has been chosen because of its modesty; the more usual style, we are told, is a low-necked gauze tunic, transparent enough to need beneath it 'un pantalon de tricot'.

une âme de boue, le ton et le langage de son état'.[7]

Pleasure gardens, balls (the dancing craze of 1797 was the waltz, imported from Germany) and theatres, provided light-hearted entertainment, a world removed from the rigorous austerity promoted by Jacobin Puritanism. Many of the theatres put on light comedies of manners in which many of the prominent types in the Directory were made fun of; obvious targets were the *muscadins* with their bizarre costume; and the *parvenus* and *nouveaux riches* with their vulgarity and pretentiousness, slipping on the polished floors of the salons as they tried to copy the manners of a more elegant age.

Beauvert's illustrated *Caricatures Politiques* (An VI) (1797–8) includes a sketch entitled *l'enrichi*, a description of a parvenu who has made money illicitly out of the new regime, and dresses in imitation of the old, in knee-breeches, white silk stockings and buckled shoes; another wealthy man is *l'acheté* (his patriotism has been bought by the government) who is shown carrying a purse – he is deaf to the cries of the poor.[8]

Beauvert's hero is the *indépendant*, (see fig. 73), the respectable property-owning republican, supporting the law and the government, and yet the true friend of the people; 'Ce sont des hommes fiers et simples, très-près de la nature'. His clothing reflects his moderate politics, in its sense of proportion and modest elegance, avoiding the extremes of affectation on the one hand, and slovenliness on the other; he wears a cutaway frock coat, 'un pantalon de drap fin ou de tricot, collé sur la cuisse et la jambe', a round hat with a tricolour cockade, and boots.[9] The elegant fake nudity of such a man's tight-fitting pantaloons was quite different from the loose, shapeless trousers of the *sans-culottes*; the *indépendant*'s clean hair and white linen (as described by Beauvert) also distinguished him from the man engaged in physical toil. Beauvert's savage *sans-culotte*, *l'exlusif* (see Chapter 3), with his 'air inquiet' and 'mauvaise humeur', his Hercules club, and his

73 *L'indépendant*, from Beauvert's *Caricatures Politiques 1797–8*.

The ideal moderate revolutionary, 'sans peur et sans reproche', wears what has become almost a uniform for the progressive middle-class man: a dark blue coat, buff waistcoat and pantaloons. A tricolour cockade is pinned to his black round hat.

coarse dirty clothing, was a nightmare figure of the very recent past.[10]

Beauvert's last *caricature politique* is the *sistématique*, the hidebound man who really regrets the Revolution, for it has brought him no profit (he had earned his money from rents which had largely fallen away). He waits for the government to fall, and although he dresses soberly, his aristocratic sympathies are shown by his green

collar (the colour of the comte d'Artois, youngest brother of Louis XVI) and the banner he holds which is decorated with gold *fleurs-de-lis*.[11]

These *caricatures politiques* include, therefore, two violently opposed viewpoints in the Directory — extreme republicanism and the no less fervent (though less obvious to view) belief in monarchy.

Jacobinism and its *sans-culotte* adherents were not quite extinguished, although as a political force they were relatively unimportant, especially after the closure of the Jacobin clubs late in 1794. During the last months of the Convention, however, they were still very much in evidence in the streets in their distinctive costume, although a popular song, 'Conseils aux sans-culottes', urged them to abandon their trousers, 'le Costume indécent de nos faux Patriotes . . .' and to return to knee-breeches.[12] It was the more politically active among this group who enforced the wearing of the cockade,[13]

---

74 *Citoyens arrêtés suspects*, attributed to Pierre-Etienne Le Sueur.

During the Terror and in the uneasy, volatile atmosphere which followed the downfall of Robespierre, it was dangerous to demonstrate anti-republican attitudes, even inadvertently, in one's costume. In this respect, not wearing the tricolour cockade, or wearing green (a colour with aristocratic overtones) counted as crimes.

Citoyen qu'on arrête pour l'obliger de mettre une cocarde Nationale à son chapeau, plusieurs ont été détenus au corps de garde pendant des heures pour avoir négligé de porter ce signe patriotique.

Citoyen arrêté comme Suspect à cause de son habit vert, de qui l'on veut voir la carte civique.

75 *Faites la paix*, c. 1797, Louis-Léopold Boilly.

The unfortunate girl tries to make peace between her two lovers, a situation exacerbated by the fact that they hold opposing political views. On the left is the *Incroyable* whose royalist inclinations are demonstrated by his formal *bicorne* hat, powdered hair, knee-breeches and pumps. The other man, with his short hair, round hat, pantaloons and boots, shows his republican sympathies.

which, in the uneasy months following the downfall of Robespierre, was the only political sign allowed on clothing. A law of 2 Prairial An III (21 May 1795) stated: 'La cocarde nationale est le seul signe de ralliement des bons citoyens: tout autre signe ou devise par écrit ou autrement sur les chapeaux, bannières ou vêtemens, est expressement défendu.' A few days later a further law (7 Prairial) stated that any individual tearing off a cockade from the clothing of another was considered to be an enemy of liberty.

Almost certainly they had in mind the antics of the *jeunesse dorée*, fashionable young men (about

115

76 *Les Incroyables*, 1797, Carle Vernet.

Caricaturists found a perfect subject in the form of the masculine fashions of the late 1790s. Both young men wear tight-fitting square-cut coats with huge lapels, and knee-breeches decorated with loops of fabric. Their political sympathies are not necessarily clear. Although their *culottes* date from the *ancien régime*, their printed cravats are working-class in origin; and, while the man on the left wears his hair plaited at the back *à la victime*, the man on the right has a revolutionary cockade prominently pinned to his hat. Both have shaggy hair, the side locks falling like spaniel's ears. The implication seems to be that fashion is more important than ideology.

two to three thousand in number, and composed mainly of middle-class youth, sons of 'suspects' and of guillotine victims) who in the aftermath of the Terror had pursued a vigorous campaign against the Jacobins. Encouraged as a political pressure group by Louis-Marie Fréron, an ex-terrorist deputy of the Convention, bands of these young men roamed the streets and public places; they erased revolutionary inscriptions on public buildings, defaced or broke the busts of republican idols like Marat, and roared out the Thermidorean song, *Le Réveil du Peuple*, drowning out the sounds of the Jacobin *Ça Ira*, and the *Marseillaise*. They tried to remove the *bonnet rouge*, the red collar, and the cockade from the

Jacobins, who in their turn attempted to tear off the black or green collars worn by the *jeunesse dorée*; Georges Duval had his collar removed in this way, and some of his friends had their hair forcibly shorn *à la Titus*,[14] a style associated with republican virility.

The accusation of effeminacy was sometimes levelled at the *jeunesse dorée*, also called the *muscadins* (a word first used in the mid eighteenth century for a scented fop, but coming into wider usage in the spring of 1793) because of their elegant clothing and freshly shaved appearance; they were a deliberate contrast to what Duval calls 'les façons grossières et la saleté officielle du costume des Jacobins'.[15]

Accounts of their costume vary slightly, but the most notable features were a greatcoat with a black or green collar, tight-fitting *culottes* reaching almost to the calf, a fiercely starched cravat, and long hair, sometimes turned up with a comb at the back in imitation, it was said, of the hair thus arranged for the blade of the guillotine. Laure Junot, future duchesse d'Abrantès, remembered Napoleon complaining about the appearance of these *muscadins*:

The young men to whom Bonaparte alluded wore grey greatcoats with black collars and green cravats. Their hair, instead of being à la Titus, which was the prevailing fashion of the day, was powdered, plaited and turned up with a comb, while on each side of the face hung two long curls called dog's-ears [oreilles de chien]. As these young men were very frequently attacked, they carried about with them large sticks which were not always merely weapons of defence, for the frays which arose in Paris at that time were often provoked by them.[16]

The elegant anarchy of their clothing, inspired by the Anglomania of the 1780s (though in an exaggerated form) was seen by their opponents as an aristocratic affectation; Philippe-Egalité had sometimes dressed as a *muscadin*, and the café de Chartres in the Palais-Egalité was the main rallying point for the *jeunesse dorée*. Very few of them

were positively royalist in their political beliefs; their actions were motivated more by dislike of the Jacobins and by desire for the freedom to be provoking in dress and manners which has always appealed to the young, especially after a time of austerity. Yet the epithets applied to them indicated a popular belief that they were, in their dress at least, sympathetic to the idea of a monarchy. François Gendron, in his book *La Jeunesse dorée* lists some of these names: '. . . collets noirs, collets verts, incroyables . . . oreilles de chien, chouants . . . messieurs à batons, Royale Cravate, Royale Anarchie . . . Fréronistes', and so on.[17]

By the end of 1795 the *jeunesse dorée* were no longer a political force and the Convention had given way to a new government, the Directory. Yet the style of costume worn by these young men was only to a minor degree influenced by their political opinions; it had a fashion life of its own, even thriving on the satire directed against it. Mercier's comments are particularly bitter, because he had hoped that young men opposed to the Jacobins would still be ardent republicans and not the somewhat effeminate crypto-royalists which many had turned out to be, 'espèce d'hommes occupés d'une parure élégante ou ridicule, qu'un coup de tambour métamorphose en femmes'.[18] Their costume, he says, is as follows:

. . . a square coat of an immeasurable length, folded over the knees; the breeches cover the calves of the legs. The shoes are stuck on to the point of the foot, and are thin as pasteboard; the head reposes on a cravat as on a cushion in form of a wash-hand basin; with others it serves as a grave for their chins.[19]

These are the men familiar to us, through the work of the caricaturists of the later 1790s, as the *Incroyables* – the word first appeared late in 1796. Unbelievable the costume may have been (it was only slightly exaggerated by the caricaturists), but its basic elegance of style, relying on excellence of fit, encouraged better tailoring. In the

77 Jean-Baptiste Isabey and his daughter, 1795, François Gérard.

Gérard was a neighbour, in the artists' quarters in the Louvre, of the miniaturist J.-B. Isabey. Isabey wears a short coat of black velvet, a black silk double-breasted waistcoat, and greyish-green cloth pantaloons; the ribbon garters just below the knee help, via loops, to support the soft leather top-boots, and they also create an illusion of knee-breeches. The artist's hair is arranged in the fashionable dishevelled 'antique' style, and in accord with the stylish simplicity of masculine costume at this period, the cravat is just a wide band of linen, lightly starched, and wound round the neck.

His small daughter wears a high-waisted cotton frock, fastening under the pleated bodice with a drawstring; it has short sleeves and a tucked hem which can be lengthened as the child grows.

first issue of the *Journal des Dames et des Modes* (1 June 1797) we read, apropos men's dress, that loose and baggy clothes are far too 'peasant-like' to be the fashion, a theme taken up later that year by the *Tableau Général du Goût, des Modes et Costumes de Paris*, which states that such negligent attire (along with over-familiar manners) is inimical to polite behaviour.[20] Although the Directory signalled a discreet return to property and privilege, there could be no possibility of turning the clock back to the days of the *ancien régime* with the silks, lace and embroideries of formal dress; muted, sober colours were the rule on all occasions.

With regard to the details of men's dress, there are few changes to chronicle during the last years of the eighteenth century. The assiduous reader of the fashion magazines (revived from 1797) comes across minor changes in dress – the height of a collar, the shape of a pocket-flap, a new method of tying a cravat, and so on – but the basic design of costume alters very little. The

Journal des Dames et des Modes (which often confesses itself at a loss to say anything new about men's fashions) notes on January 1799 that the everyday costume worn by the *élégant* is a coat or frock of black, cut away at the front and with metal buttons; it is worn with pantaloons and boots, for shoes and knee-breeches are only to be seen at balls.

Adding a little detail to that, we can say that dark colours generally were preferred for the coat, which could be single- or double-breasted and had tails at the back. Using the finest broadcloths (greatly improved with the introduction of fine Spanish merino wool) the expert tailor moulded and defined the body with a well-cut coat, so that it fitted to perfection. Long, tight-fitting breeches or pantaloons also demanded high-quality tailoring, especially when legs were less than perfect; the quasi-nude look created by buff-coloured pantaloons which hugged the limbs proved sometimes more risible than nobly antique.

With the coat and pantaloons (or breeches), men wore a light-coloured *veste* or *gilet*; the word *gilet* was sometimes used for the upper waistcoat, for by the late 1790s two were often worn, of different lengths and colours. Waistcoats, too, could be double- or single-breasted like the coat, and their main focus of interest was the large lapels, which framed, as it were, an expanse of starched white cravat and linen shirt ruffle. The *redingote* could either be a fairly tight-fitting coat or a more voluminous garment with a caped collar. Men with artistic tastes, according to a fashion journal of 1799, could wear a *redingote* rather like a gown in shape, with a roll collar; it fastened with frogging at the front, and it had black 'antique' embroidery at the hem.[21] Artistic men, or those who wished to escape from what they saw as a boring uniformity in dress, could swathe themselves in a cloak, a garment which revived in popularity in the late 1790s, ironically enough just a few years after David had failed to make it essential wear, *à l'antique*, for the republi-

78 *Portrait of a young man, c.* 1797(?), Jean-Baptiste Greuze.

The identity of this elegant young man has not been firmly established. He is sometimes called Louis Antoine de Saint-Just (the revolutionary leader was famed for the elegance of his clothing), but the presence, on the right, of a copy of the Belvedere Mercury (the original was brought to the Louvre in 1797 as part of the Italian booty) may rule this out.

The name most recently proposed is that of Talleyrand's nephew, Auguste-Louis de Talleyrand.

The costume is that of a fashionable young man, probably in sympathy with the ideals of the Revolution, and dates from the mid to late 1790s. The dark coat, double-breasted waistcoat, buff pantaloons and boots are the stock-in-trade of the middle-class and intellectual republican, as are the classical references.

79 *Madame Emilie Sériziat*, 1795, Jacques-Louis David.

Painted in the uneasy months after the end of the Terror, Madame Sériziat's costume is a mixture of the stylish and the simple. Her chemise dress with its plain drawstring neck, and her kerchief, are of white cotton, modestly opaque; at her waist is a green silk sash. Over her lace-edged muslin cap, she wears an elegant straw hat, the crown covered in green silk ribbon; a sign of the changing times is the tiny cockade almost hidden under the bow.

can citizen. Dark in colour, capacious in cut, and dramatic in movement, the cloak of the end of the century now gave its wearer the air of a Romantic hero. This effect was further emphasized by the carefully arranged wildness of the hair, cut short in a variety of 'natural' styles; natural it may have been compared to the powdered wig of the *ancien régime*, but it required the art of a skilful hairdresser to cut and curl the hair, producing an elegantly negligent appearance. (Byron once confessed to a friend that his hair had to be 'curled naturally every night', but begged him not to reveal this weakness.) By the late 1790s, the fashion magazines report that the most popular hairstyle for men was the Titus, which had (in France, at least[22]) become more fashionable than republican. If a hat was worn at all, it was usually the English round hat, although ultra-fashionable young men like the *Incroyables* occasionally chose to wear a kind of bicorne hat, *à l'androsmane*, turned up sharply in the front and the back.

At the risk of over-simplification, the *Incroyables* can be seen as one of those manifestations of masculine defiance against the sartorial uniformity which they think is being imposed on them; the dandies were the last genuine movement of this kind in the nineteenth century – apart from artistic dress reform movements, which had little impact outside their own groups. Otherwise, we are, in the late eighteenth century, on the brink of what J. C. Flügel calls the 'Great Masculine Renunciation'[23] – that is, the rejection of finery in place of costume dictated above all by the work ethic. If we look at the fashion magazines of the period (and at the work of later historians of dress) we see a scene in which women are the dominating force. This had not been the case during the eighteenth century as a whole (when the costume of *both* sexes was a subject for intelligent discussion), or during the Revolution itself (when, if anything, the question of what men wore, or should wear, was more important than any consideration of women's fashions).

80 *Woman and child, c.* 1795–6, François-André Vincent.

The mother wears a simple morning costume consisting of a short frilled bodice and skirt of white cotton. Elegant touches, in honour of the portrait, are the white silk hair ribbon imitating a classical bandeau, and a purple silk fringed shawl draped asymmetrically *à l'antique*. Her daughter wears a white cotton dress, embroidered at the hem with a bright floral design.

The Goncourts took the view that as men had produced the tyranny of the Terror, it was women who brought about the Thermidorean reaction, or at least promoted in their costume and manners a fierce blacklash against the excesses of Robespierre's Republic of Virtue. One of the most spectacular forms of reaction were the *bals des victimes* in the months after 9 Thermidor; 'La France danse. Elle danse depuis thermidor; elle danse comme elle chantait autrefois; elle danse pour se venger, elle danse pour oublier. Entre son passé sanglant, son avenir sombre, elle danse . . .'[24]

To begin with, mourning was worn at these balls: 'il fallait être en grand deuil pour avoir le droit de paraître et de danser, en souvenir des personnes chères qu'on regrettait et que la Terreur avait immolées'.[25] In chilling mockery of the Terror (or did they mock themselves for having succumbed to such horror?), some of the dancers had their hair cut *à la victime*, and wore red shawls in recollection of those thrown over murderers when executed – 'ce meme châle que Samson avait jeté sur les blanches épaules de Charlotte Corday . . . allant a l'échafaud'.[26] In defiance of the recent orgy of blood-letting under the Terror, some women wore a red ribbon round the neck in imitation of the cut made by the blade of the guillotine;[27] this somewhat sinister theme continued into the late 1790s when there was a fashion for scarlet ribbons crossed over the bodice

of women's dress, such *croisures à la victime* indicating that their wearers would sacrifice everything for their lovers.[28]

After these sartorial protests, women began to adopt the most extreme forms of 'classical' costume in defiance both of Jacobin Puritanism and conventional morality. In the winter of 1794–5,

81 *Fashion plate*, 1798, from the *Journal des Dames et des Modes.*

Her hair tied up in a kerchief (a fashion lingering from the working-class styles worn during the height of the Revolution), this *élégante* wears a high-waisted muslin robe, the bodice decorated with 'croisures à la victime'.

Mercier recalled, the costume worn at public balls (hundreds of dance halls had opened in Paris) was so extraordinary that it was almost impossible to believe that the Terror was only just over. His famous description is worth quoting at length:

Here lighted lustres reflect their splendour on beauties dressed à la Cléopatre, à la Diane, à la Psyché; there, a smoky lamp sheds its oily beams on a troop of washerwomen who dance in wooden shoes, with their muscadins, to the noise of some sorry scraper. I know not whether the first of these dancers have any great affection for the republican forms of the Grecian governments, but they have modelled the form of their dress after that of Aspasia [fifth century BC Greek courtesan and mistress of Pericles]; *bare arms, naked breasts, feet shod with sandals, hair turned in tresses around their heads by modish hairdressers, who study the antique busts. Guess where are the pockets of these dancers? They have none; they stick their fan in their belt, and lodge in their bosom a slight purse of morocco leather in which are a few spare guineas. As to the ignoble handkerchief, it is in the pocket of some courtier, to whom they address themselves in case of need. The shift has long since been banished, as it seemed only to spoil the contours of nature; and besides, it was an inconvenient part of dress ... The flesh-coloured knit-work silk stays, which stuck close*

---

82 *Portrait of a young woman, c.* 1800, circle of Jacques-Louis David.

That the caricaturists did not exaggerate too much in their depiction of the semi-nude fashions of the late 1790s, can be seen in this portrait, where the gossamer-thin muslin of the upper bodice reveals the nipples quite clearly. The austerity of the portrait (the artist may have been a pupil of David) echoes the neoclassical simplicity of the sitter's costume, the plain white cotton dress, the fringed shawl, and the plait of hair wound round the top of the head in imitation of an antique bandeau.

83 *Madame Elisabeth Dunoyer*, 1797, Jean-Baptiste François Desoria.

Seated on an 'antique' chair, Madame Dunoyer is depicted in the simplest of neo-classical costume, a high-waisted cotton chemise gown with drawstring neck and waist; her short curls, *à la Titus*, are threaded with a ribbon bandeau.

---

to the body did not leave the beholder to divine, but perceive, every secret charm. This is what was called being dressed à la sauvage, and the women dressed in this manner during a rigorous winter, in spite of frost and snow.[29]

Semi-nude and dressed in white – 'toutes les femmes sont en blanc et le blanc sied à toutes les femmes'[30] – such women danced with abandon, and with almost a religious ecstasy. The often transparent dress revealed the shape of the body, which, as Mercier implies, was barely covered with underwear; as well as the knitted stays which he describes, some women wore flesh-coloured tights,[31] although this was thought rather indecent. White in colour, revealing in design, neo-classical dress in its most extreme form – a beguiling mixture of fake innocence and eroticism – perfectly enhanced the charms of *demi-mondaine* leaders of society like Thérèse Tallien; 'Notre Dame de Thermidor' (it was mainly to save her that Tallien set in motion the events that led to the fall of Robespierre) was one of the leaders of the *Merveilleuses*, feminine counterparts of the *Incroyables*. Her stylish toilettes were greatly admired, one outfit in 1796 attracting particular acclaim; it

... consisted of a plain robe of India muslin, draped in the antique style, and fastened at the shoulders by two cameos; a gold belt encircled her waist, and was likewise fastened by a cameo; a broad gold bracelet confined her sleeve considerably above the elbow; her hair, of a glossy black, was short and frizzed all round her head, in the fashion then called à la Titus; over her fair and finely turned shoulders was thrown a superb red cachemire shawl, an article at that time very rare and in great request. She disposed it around her in a manner at once graceful and picturesque.[32]

The affected and expensive simplicity of this dress (India muslin was very expensive) was set off by a fine shawl, which women of fashion knew how to drape in the most becoming style. Such shawls (a fashion taken from the English, noted the *Journal de la Mode et du Goût* in June 1790) could be transformed into a variety of classical mantles. The *Tableau Général du Goût, des Modes et Costumes de Paris*, late in 1799, remarked that in some of the most exclusive gatherings it was the fashion for women to wear pleated tunics resembling the Roman *stola*, and a *palla*, or Roman mantle draped over the left shoulder;[33] Louise Fusil also recalled a cloth mantle, embroidered in gold and thrown over one shoulder.[34] It was soft, supple cashmere which was thought to drape best in the antique style; Josephine Beauharnais was devoted to shawls made from this highly prized material, which she wore with unequalled grace. Charming rather than beautiful, and expert in capturing hearts (in the spring of 1796 she married the young General Bonaparte), Josephine's expense on clothes was prodigal; along with Mesdames Tallien and Récamier, she was one of the leaders of Directory society – they were inevitably called the Three Graces when seen together dressed *à l'antique*.

These great 'ladies' were the leaders of some sixty to eighty *élégantes*, whose *toilettes* inspired the fashions detailed in the *Journal des Dames et des Modes* which began in June 1797: 'Ce sont elles que nous suivons aux spectacles, aux bals, aux promenades, c'est leur costume copié, avec la plus exacte précision, que nous donnons pour modèle.'[35] The editor was keen to emphasize that the costumes he depicted came from the best society, in case the less sophisticated of his readers, amazed at the daring nature of some of the outfits, accused him of using ladies of dubious virtue as models.

The fashionable pleasure gardens of Tivoli and Frascati were fruitful hunting grounds for those in search of the latest modes. The most popular costume to be seen at Tivoli, according to Louise Fusil, was a dress of white muslin embroidered in arabesques of coloured wool, and tied at the waist with a sash.[36] Arnault also recollected 'des longues tuniques de mousseline ou de percale blanche, ornées de bandes ou de broderies en laine (on avait horreur de la soie)'.[37] The fashion for white cottons led to greater cleanliness in dress, and – since more of the body was revealed – in the person; 'an elegant woman did not pass two days without bathing', said the duchesse d'Abrantès.

'It was then the fashion for the ladies' dresses to fall like the draperies of the antique statues',[38] a style given further encouragement by the popularity of the art of classical antiquity; since 1793 this had been available for the public to study in the Louvre, and from 1798 the state collections were immensely enriched by the arrival of booty from Italy, including many great works of classical art. As Mercier said, white suited all women, and dress in the neo-classical style – the ubiquitous chemise – was a favourite among nearly all women: 'Not a *petite maîtresse*, not a *grisette*, who

84 *Madame Juliette Récamier*, 1800, Jacques-Louis David.

Madame Récamier, reclining on the 'antique' chaise-longue which was one of the props in David's studio, disliked this portrayal of her as – in the words of the duchesse d'Abrantès – 'a beautiful marble statue, silent and cold'; when the artist refused to alter it, it remained unsold and unfinished. One of the great, spoilt beauties of the Directoire and Consulate, Madame Récamier poses, bare-footed, in the high-waisted white gown so indispensable an aid to the cultivation of the classical ambience.

does not decorate herself on Sunday with an Athenian muslin gown, and who does not draw up the pendant folds on the right arm, in order to drop into the form of some antique or at least equal Venus *aux belles fesses.*'[39] The clinging draperies of such a gown not only revealed the buttocks (we can here override the coyness of Mercier's English translator), but emphasized the breast; in addition, the waist of the dress, from the mid 1790s, grew higher and higher until by the end of the century it was right under the bust.

In ultra-fashionable circles (and especially among the *demi-mondaines*) the chemise gown, according to the *Journal des Dames et des Modes* (10 April 1798) was sleeveless and cut very low in the front and at the back. In terms of dress, this was the closest that the late eighteenth century could get to the flowing drapery seen on Greek vases and statues (in the hedonistic world of the Directory, the sensuality of Greece was preferred to the austerity of Rome). This was undoubtedly one of the reasons why Madame Récamier preferred her lively portrait by Gérard (1805) to the cold, aloof image which David presented of her in 1800. In David's famous portrait (see fig. 84) she wears the more modest and structured form of the chemise, with a bodice lined to give support to the bust, and the short sleeves set in deeply, to give the narrow back which had distinguished the dresses of the eighteenth century. Apart from the ultra-classical style (the true chemise was a simple tube of material slipped over the head and fastened with a sash at the waist), the more fitted gowns had a bodice cut separately from the skirt and joined at the waist, with a variety of front fastenings; a number of surviving dresses of the late 1790s have a small pad attached to the rear of the bodice, supporting the gathered pleats of the skirt folds – a slight echo of the bouncy back draperies of the 1780s.

Most women on everyday occasions were modest in appearance, in spite of the reputation of the Directory for licentious clothing. When the more classical gown was worn with its softly pleated draperies, a long-waisted underbodice gave some support to the body; as we have seen, the tight, high-waisted and more fitted dress had its own built-in support in the bodice. In addition, the climate of Paris was not always suitable for revealing the body in the way it was thought the ancients did. Since it was easy for bare arms to get chapped and weather-beaten, knitted flesh-coloured silk sleeves were sometimes added to a sleeveless dress; these could then be removed for the evening.

Fashion magazines and portraits of the time give the impression that the antique style was all the rage. To a great extent this was true – far more so than in England where the purity of the classical line was often diluted with fussy decoration or the kind of historical features which Englishwomen have always loved. But it must be stated that women wore fabrics other than white muslin. Although by 1800 there were only about 2000 silk workshops in Lyons, plain light-coloured taffetas and silks with tiny patterns continued to be produced for more formal dresses; colourful printed cottons and linens were also fashionable for informal wear. Again, although the pages of the fashion magazines are dominated by gowns of the 'classical' type, other dresses (the occasional open robe, or a *demi-habillement* – a tunic or short robe worn over a round gown) also appear.

Since it was not always appropriate or practical for women to float around like Athenian goddesses, more functional garments were needed in the fashionable wardrobe. For winter, in particular, *douillettes* (indoor coat-dresses with long sleeves) were worn, and out of doors women wore riding costumes, and *redingotes*. In the 1780s and during the early years of the Revolution, jacket and skirt styles had been particularly popular; they were at the same time tactfully 'democratic' and flattering to the tiny waist then in fashion. By the late 1790s, when the waist was very high, the most fashionable jacket was the spencer, which (in spite of its fashionable

85 *Portrait of a girl, c.* 1800, Jean-Auguste-Dominique Ingres.

The sitter, possibly Barbara Bansi, poses against an unidentified southern landscape; the balloon and parachute derive from a popular print depicting the exploits of Jacques Garnerin who made a number of parachute jumps over Paris in the late 1790s. The dress, so constructed that the very high waist supports the bust, has short sleeves made of dimity, a cotton with a small raised pattern.

The arrangement of the fine cashmere shawl shows off elegantly shaped arms and a white skin, as does the knotted silk bracelet. Her feet are shod in *cothurnes*, and the classical effect is further enhanced by the hair with its bunch of curls at the back *à l'antique*, tendrils forming a fringe, and a plait acting as a bandeau.

(71)

English name coined in 1789) derived from the *pierrot* or the *caraco* of that period. The spencer was clearly not a classical garment, although the fashionable 'Anglo-grecque' ladies of the 'Petit Coblentz' – that is, the boulevard des Italiens, a royalist meeting place – sometimes wore such garments with small sleeves 'à la romaine'.[40] The decoration of the spencer provided an opportunity for designs other than the classical, and trimmings in the military style – frogged fastenings and looped braids – were particularly popular. French military successes were reflected also in headwear, the most sensitive barometer of the mood of the times, according to the editor of the *Journal des Dames et des Modes*. In the issue of 1 November, 1798, apropos Napoleon's Egyptian compaigns, he notes that the modistes are making 'des bonnets en crocodiles'; having heard that Egyptian themes are all the rage in London also, he complains tongue-in-cheek: 'Nous seuls pouvions disposer du Nil, des pyramides, et des crocodiles.' The Egyptian expedition also produced a fashion for turbans, part of that fascina-

86 *Fashion plate*, 1798, from the *Journal des Dames et des Modes*.

Seen from the back, this fashionable lady wears a sleeveless braided spencer over a plain muslin gown; both the spencer and the turban are described as *à l'algérienne*. She carries a *reticule* or *ridicule*, an indispensable accessory of the period; there were, according to the editor of the *Journal*, 'des ridicules du matin, des ridicules de sociétés, des ridicules de bals, des ridicules de spectacles'.

tion with the Orient which had inspired French dress throughout the eighteeenth century.

Fashion thrives on variety and not on uniformity; it was expressed most of all in the different types of head-dress available to the readers of the fashion journals. The fairly simple bonnets of the early 1790s gave way, by the end of the decade, to a multitude of styles; these included elaborately trimmed hats, military style *casques* (inspired by classical helmets), *toques* and *capotes* (bonnets with a soft gathered crown and large brim) – there is hardly a cockade to be seen among them, so removed from high fashion did this reminder of the Revolution appear by the late 1790s. By this time, many *élégantes* opted for hats which recalled the romantic past, feather-trimmed velvet caps, for example; this was part of the movement towards the arts of the Middle Ages and the Renaissance[41] known as *le style troubadour* (a term invented later by Théophile Gautier), which was encouraged by Josephine Bonaparte as both patron of artists and leader of fashion. Such historical romanticism, however, did not really break loose until the Empire; during the Directory it made little headway against the prevailing popularity of the classical look.

This classical style inspired not only a distinctive dress, but complementary accessories, and a new freedom in movement. The flowing, natural lines of the dress of classical antiquity demanded, ideally, bare feet; since this would be impractical, feet were shod in *cothurnes* which the *Journal des Dames et des Modes* described as 'des sandales attachées avec des rubans qui s'entrelaçent élégamment autour de la jambe', or in flat pumps. Such footwear aided vigorous movement, quite unlike 'the peculiarly bad, unsteady walk, something between a trip and a totter, that Frenchwomen of rank used to acquire from their high heels and the habit of never using their feet'.[42]

Another transformation which the new style of dress brought about was the introduction of the handbag to contain those essentials – money, keys, mirror, cosmetics, handkerchief and fan – which the woman of fashion needed about her person. Under the more voluminous gowns of the pre-Revolutionary period such items were carried in pockets which hung from the waist but they were impossible to wear with the clinging dresses of the Directory. Mercier tells us that the scantily dressed *sauvages* carried a purse pushed into the front of their bodice when dancing. A more practical solution was for women to carry their valuables in a small bag that hung from the wrist, and derived from the silk drawstring bag in which a lady kept her implements for knotting, a fashionable pastime of the earlier eighteenth century. Such *réticules* (they were sometimes mocked as *ridicules*) proved to be more popular than an alternative kind of bag, the *balantine*, which hung from the waist – not only was this too reminiscent of the old pocket, but it broke up the flowing line of the classical gown.

The tendency towards uniformity in neoclassical dress has already been noted; one of the signs of a true *élégante* was to demonstrate individual taste in the elegance of her accessories. As luxury was back in fashion by the late 1790s, what better way to show off wealth than by a display of jewellery? Naked arms (and feet, too, if we are to believe Mercier) glittered with diamonds on the extravagant social occasions of the Directory. More in the antique taste, however, were cameos, engraved gems, and semi-precious stones like turquoise, which could decorate the combs and bandeaux worn by ladies of fashion in their hair.

Such hair ornaments looked their best on long hair, which could be worn in a number of ways. Although short hair in the popular classical styles – such as the Titus and the Caracalla – was to be seen in many of the fashion plates, it was rather limiting. To solve this problem, a wardrobe of wigs could effect instant transformations; according to Mercier, women of fashion ordered wigs as they ordered shoes, and might have as many as forty.[43] As well as the short wigs, there were

87 *Un salon parisien sous le Directoire, c.* 1799, Jean-François Bosio.

This satire on the exaggerated fashions and raffish manners of society under the Directory is typical of caricatures of the period, confirming the worst opinions of the puritanical Jacobins, that licence and debauchery reigned in the relaxed atmosphere of the new regime. Ladies, dressed in the extremes of the neo-classical style, reveal their charms, offering obvious incitement to their amorous masculine companions.

In a society suspended between republican manners and a revival of *ancien régime* etiquette, contemporaries noted the diversity in classes thronging the salons of the Directory; here, for example, can be seen both former revolutionaries in tousled hair and trousers or pantaloons, and an aristocrat in powdered hair and formal suit with knee-breeches.

longer versions; the *Miroir* for 29 Thermidor An VI (16 August 1797) commented on the protean 'perruque grecque' which could trail over the neck, be dressed in a chignon at the back of the head, or be knotted on the top. Like any other item of dress, the wig was subject to the caprice of fashion; blond wigs, for example, were all the rage in the spring of 1796, and the gossip column of one of the Paris newspapers, *L'Ami des Lois*, notes:

The story is being told in the Paris salons, as if it were a remarkable event, of the change in coiffure of mesdames Tallien and Buonaparte. Both had long been distinguished for their superb black tresses; but at last they have been compelled to yield to the craze for blond wigs. A woman with black hair would be painfully conspicuous in good society.[44]

Such a story, if the authorities bothered to read it, might cause amusement or mild head-shaking at the frivolity of women, but no more – after all, the ladies mentioned were under the highest protection. Yet the Directors were aware how slight was their hold on a public whose political allegiance over the last few years had veered from one extreme to another; Mercier observed that 'le peuple de Paris ... boit, rit, chante, danse, et murmure après un gouvernement paisible et vigilant, qu'il accuse le matin d'être royaliste, le soir d'être terroriste ...'[45] Plots, both of the right and the left, might be signalled by dress, and prevented by a vigilant police, a force which had multiplied during the Revolution and especially during the Terror when the government had been obsessed with gossip and rumour as indications of possible subversion. In the aftermath of the Terror, the government had to cope with gang warfare between the Jacobins and the *jeunesse dorée* – factions as divided in dress as they were in political beliefs. Fearing that the activities of the *jeunesse dorée* and their supporters might herald a serious counter-revolutionary upheaval, the police kept a wary eye on such evidence of royalist sympathies as, for example, the wearing

of white Bourbon badges or *fleurs-de-lis*.[46] It was also sensible to note what women were wearing and to take the advice of the editor of the *Journal des Dames et des Modes*; 'Voulez-vous connaître l'esprit public, le goût dominant, ou la nouvelle du jour? Examinez la toilette de nos aimables Parisiennes ...'

The evidence was somewhat conflicting. Counter-revolutionary signs included fans and sweet-boxes decorated with *fleurs-de-lis*,[47] white plumes worn at the threatre, and a sighting, in the Jardins d'Egalité in May 1797 of 'une robe à la Bourbon ... parsemée de fleurs de lis très petites'.[48] Possibly the wearer of this dress had hoped to escape detection, as the design was so small. Women were also seen to wear jewelled chains with eighteen links, a sign perhaps of support for the comte de Provence who had, in June 1795, proclaimed himself Louis XVIII; if questioned, however, the astute wearer could claim that her chain referred to the coup of 18 Fructidor (4 September 1797) by which the Directory suppressed a royalist plot.

On the other hand, the temporary revival of Jacobin fortunes in the late summer of 1797 gave birth to a number of styles *à la Marat*. The *Miroir* noted the popularity of 'bandeaux à la Marat', adding the pious hope: 'C'est sans doute pour réveiller notre indignation contre les Jacobins que les dames nous en montrent de temps en temps la livrée, et par là, rapellent à notre souvenir les horreurs qu'ils nous ont fait souffrir.'[49] Later that year the *Journal des Dames et des Modes* (10 November) showed a turban-like kerchief which it named a 'fichu à la Marat', after the swathed white head-dress which he wore 'quand il fut assassiné dans sa baignoire', and which, claimed the editor, was a popular style during the Terror.

What did the authorities make of these sartorial foibles, so diligently recorded? Probably very little, for no action seems to have been taken. It was acknowledged that the political situation was not too stable and could change at any moment; provided that public order was not outraged by too deliberate a provocation (which could just as easily be caused by the immodest toilettes of the *élégantes*, as by censured political symbols), fashion was allowed to go its own way. It would have done so in any case, for it obeyed only its own mysterious laws. It is useless to rail against the tyranny of fashion, says the *Journal des Dames et des Modes*: 'la mode ... triomphe des indifférens qui la négligent, ou des envieux qui ne peuvent l'atteindre ... elle naît je ne sais où, elle est maintenue par je ne sais qui, et finit je ne sais comment'.

5 | Postscript

Citizens, the Revolution is established upon the principles which began it: it is ended.

Proclamation of 24 Frimaire, An VIII (15 December 1799)

Bedevilled by constitutional problems and increasingly reliant on the army to keep it in power, the Directory fell victim to Napoleon's ambition in the *coup d'état* of 18 Brumaire, 1799. Furious at French reverses abroad (nearly all his Italian conquests had been lost), aware of France's internal problems and eager to profit from the situation, Napoleon had hastily left Egypt, arriving at Fréjus, in the south of France, early in October 1799. With a talent for dramatic effects which he never lost, he cleverly reminded the public of the successes of his Egyptian campaign by appearing in Paris in Mameluke costume, 'large white trousers, red boots, waistcoat richly embroidered, as also the jacket which was of crimson velvet'.[1]

His assumption of power a few weeks later was not, however, as smooth as later Napoleonic legend has it. When the Council of Five Hundred (the legislative councils had been summoned to meet at St Cloud outside Paris on the pretext of danger from a Jacobin uprising) dared to question Napoleon's claim that the government was in jeopardy, uproar ensued until the arrival of troops with naked bayonets. Then, 'incommoded by their togas, and holding their classic headgear in their hand, the discomfited deputies dispersed into the woods, where many of them, in order to escape the pursuit of the soldiers, left behind them these melancholy symbols of departed dignity'.[2]

Enough of the legislators were later brought back to join the Ancients in declaring – with a faint pretence of legality – an end to the Directory. A new constitution, proclaimed in mid-December, stated that France was to be governed by three Consuls, the most important being Napoleon, whose pre-eminence was confirmed, early in 1800, by his election as First Consul.

It had been clear well before the events of 18 Brumaire, that Napoleon's ambitions encompassed more than military glory. 'Do you think I triumph in Italy to make the greatness of the lawyers of the Directory?' was the rhetorical question he put to Miot de Melito as they walked in the gardens of Mombello in 1797. To the public at large, however, these aspirations were hidden; to Mercier (who knew him as a fellow-member of the *Institut de France*) he appeared at first to be the model for all true Republicans to follow.[3]

He was certainly republican – almost Jacobin – in the negligence of his costume when the future duchesse d'Abrantès first met him during the Directory; he had, she said, 'the look of a sloven'. She remembered him in 1795 'with a shabby round hat drawn over his forehead, and ... ill-powdered hair hanging over the collar of his greatcoat', which was 'very plainly made, buttoned up to his chin'.[4]

While republican simplicity could be thought appropriate – even commendable – for the soldier, it did not project the right image for the ruler. Authority at the highest level needed to be reinforced by costume of particular splendour, and accordingly one of Napoleon's first decrees at the end of December 1799 (9 Nivôse An VIII) was to establish the costume that he and his two colleagues should wear. As with the previous regime, it was decided that two costumes were

88 *The coup d'état of 19 Brumaire 1799*, engraved by Dupréel after Jean Duplessi-Bertaux, from *Tableaux Historiques de la Révolution Française*, 1817.

The scene is the remodelled *orangerie* at Saint-Cloud where the Five Hundred in their red 'antique' mantles protest at the intrusion of Bonaparte (centre) in their midst. The general's younger brother, Lucien, conveniently in the chair, saved the situation by calling in the grenadiers, who then expelled the deputies by force.

needed, one for everyday and one for more formal occasions; again, following the example of the Directors, the colours chosen – red, white and blue – were the colours of the Revolution. The ordinary costume consisted of a blue, easy-fitting coat (*habit dégagé*) with a gold-fringed red sash and white pantaloons; the formal costume was a red coat embroidered in gold palmettes, a blue sash, and gold-embroidered white pantaloons.

Absolute power, however, enabled Napoleon to disregard these sumptuary regulations when it suited him, and to demonstrate his superiority over the other two consuls:

He had decreed for himself and his two colleagues, that on all occasions of grand ceremonial, each should wear a red coat made of velvet in winter, in summer of some other material and embroidered in gold. The two Consuls, Cambacérès and Lebrun, elderly, powdered and well set-up, wore this gorgeous coat with lace ruffles and a sword after the old fashion of full dress; but Bonaparte, who detested all such ornaments, got rid of them as much as possible . . . With his crimson and gold coat he would wear a black cravat, a lace frill to his shirt but no sleeve ruffles. Sometimes he wore a

137

Buonaparte, l'an IV.

89 *'Buonaparte, l'an IV'*, c. 1796, attributed to Jean-Baptiste Isabey.

Drawn when Napoleon (though the man to watch, according to the perceptive) was fairly new to great affairs of state and elegant society, Isabey's caricature shows the future ruler of France cutting a rather eccentric figure. His costume is a curious mixture of the military (his hat), the revolutionary (the cockade) and the would-be-fashionable (the wide-lapelled square-cut coat, new-style trousers cut rather short, and boots).

90 *Bonaparte as First Consul*, 1801–2, Antoine-Jean Gros.

In this flattering portrait of the First Consul – his elegant pose quite removed from what Talleyrand described as his 'camp habits' – we see Napoleon in his official costume, regally pointing to his military and political achievements. He wears a red silk double-breasted coat (*habit dégagé*) trimmed with gold embroidery, close-fitting white pantaloons also embroidered in gold, and tasselled hussar boots.

white vest embroidered in silver, but more frequently his uniform waistcoat, his uniform sword, breeches, silk stockings and boots.[5]

This carefree confusion of costumes was a clever demonstration of the unity of Napoleon's two roles; that of ruler of the state, and that of military hero. It can also be seen as indicative of a society in transition – 'It was not exactly a court', said the Princess Dolguruki, 'but it was no longer a camp.'[6]

Barrack-room behaviour, rough and ready republican manners – these were no longer tolerated, except in a few of Napoleon's closest intimates. Just as the titles 'citoyen/citoyenne' had given way, by 1800, to 'Monsieur/Madame', so the free-and-easy informality of the Directory gave way to the ritual and ceremony of what was a court in embryo under the Consulate. In 1800, the First Consul's residence was established in the former royal palace of the Tuileries; lessons in court etiquette were given by returned *émigrés*, and by former royal servants, such as Marie-Antoinette's dancing master. Returning to Paris in 1802, Miot de Melito found that:

What little had remained of austere Republican forms at the time of my departure from the capital had now disappeared. Gorgeous liveries, sumptuous garments similar to those worn in the reign of Louis XV had succeeded to the military fashions which, during the Revolution, had been adopted even in the dress of civilians. No more boots, sabres or cockades; these were replaced by tights and silk stockings, buckled shoes, dress-swords, and hats held under the arm.[7]

As though to emphasize his regal aspirations, from 1802 Napoleon (now Consul for Life) often wore the *habit à la française*, the coat with a high straight collar and sharply sloping sides which would have been worn at the court of Louis XVI; *culottes*, too, increasingly replaced pantaloons in his wardrobe (they were in any case more flattering to those with a tendency towards embonpoint), and were worn exclusively after 1805.[8]

By that time, Napoleon was Emperor and the creator of the most elaborate system of court and official dress ever put into practice.[9] This included court dress for women, the fabrics (although not the styles) imitating those of the *ancien régime* – the rich silks and glittering embroideries of French manufacture.

With the establishment of a court and a return to the ceremony and splendour associated with the *ancien régime*, was Napoleon trying to put the clock back? The answer, of course, is no, for as he said, he was the child of the Revolution. While the French people, after the insecurities of the Directory, were prepared to accept (in the guise of a monarchical system if necessary) a strong and disciplined society, there could be no return to the old world pre-1789, whose very existence was bound up in privilege and the class system. Whether France was ruled by a Bonaparte or a restored Bourbon, there could never be any doubt that a revolution had taken place, with reverberating political and social consequences.

Dress, as the most visible form of communication within society, was bound to be affected. As we have seen, there were attempts during the most radical years of the Revolution to control society by dress, as a logical extension of republican propaganda; these failed, but left their legacy in the form of a wide-ranging system of civil uniform, far more comprehensive than anything envisaged in the *ancien régime*.

In contrast to the fairly stately progress of fashion during most of the eighteenth century, the French Revolution quickened the pace of change. In some respects, it acted as a catalyst for styles already in the pipeline, but which were pushed to the forefront by the impact of politics. The trousers of the *sans-culottes*, for example, a long-established form of working-class costume, were identified with a political group, and assumed symbolic importance; during the nineteenth century, this sign of the worker became the garment worn by men of all classes. In the same way, the sober tailored costume (inspired by English styles) of the enlightened middle class of the 1780s was precisely that worn by the revolutionaries as a contrast to aristocratic foppery; the dreary uniformity of much of men's dress during the nineteenth century owes its origin to the notion that dark clothing was identified with a work ethic.

Inspired by the relative simplicities of English country clothing, the Revolution linked woollen materials, and washable cottons and linens – fabrics more easily available to the less well-off – with democracy; true republicans had supposedly less luxurious tastes than indolent, silk-clad aristocrats.

For most of the eighteenth century there was a sartorial harmony in the dress of men and women; they were united in their love of colour, elegant design and luxurious materials. One of the results of the French Revolution was to divide the sexes in terms of their clothing. Men's dress becomes plain in design and sober in colour; it is unadorned with decoration. It symbolizes *gravitas* and an indifference to luxury – essential elements of republican austerity; its virtual uniformity emphasizes the revolutionary ideal of equality. Women's dress, on the other hand – after a necessary flirtation with republican simplicity during the Terror – becomes ultra-feminine. I take this to mean costume which enhances the body and shows off the taste and status of the wearer by luxurious fabrics and accessories – dress which often indicates a life of pleasure and comparative idleness. It also signals, perhaps, the fact that women channelled some of their energy into the arts of fashion, since they were denied a political voice. The Revolution and its ideals were those of men; women had played only a minor role in the great events of 1789 and after, and their attitudes, as expressed in dress, are often unclear. We can never be sure how far their fashions, as we see them, were merely sartorial comment on topical events, a reaction to intolerable tensions, or evidence of a deep concern with the political questions of the day.

The French Revolution (like the Russian Revolution) was one of the most violent upheavals of modern times; such events force people to re-shape their lives and their thoughts, and society can never be the same again. At no other time in the history of fashion has dress been so influenced by politics, as during the French Revolution. Not only did it respond to particular political events with enthusiasm, hostility or caution – depending on the viewpoint of the wearer – but, more ominously, it was used as propaganda, in the enforcement of the ideals of liberty, equality and fraternity.

The French Revolution banished the notion that clothing was the symbol of an immutable class system based on unjust privilege. It introduced a new idea – however imperfectly realized – that dress was above all a statement of freedom and an expression of individuality.

Notes

1 The waiting years

1. *The Correspondence of William Augustus Miles on the French Revolution 1789–1817*, ed. C. P. Miles, London, 2 vols, 1890, II, p. 9.

2. C. Brinton, *A Decade of Revolution 1789–1799*, New York 1934, p. 143.

3. See D. L. Dowd, 'The French Revolution and the Painters', in *French Historical Studies*, vol. I, No. 2, 1959.

4. F. Braudel, *Civilization and Capitalism 15th to 18th Century*, London, 3 vols, 1981, I *The Structures of Everyday Life*, p. 323.

5. The *Cabinet des Modes* changed its title in November 1786; the new title recognized the importance of English as well as French fashions, and more particularly acknowledged its debt to the London publication, *The Fashionable Magazine*, which first appeared in June 1786 and lasted until December of the same year. See M. J. Ghering van Ierlant, 'Anglo-French Fashion, 1786', in *Costume*, No. 17, 1983.

6. *Journal des Dames et des Modes*, Paris 1 June 1912, p. 1.

7. Braudel, op. cit., p. 479.

8. L.-S. Mercier, *Tableau de Paris*, Amsterdam, 8 vols, 1782–8, III, p. 300: 'Naître à Paris, c'est être deux fois Français, car on y reçoit, en naissant, une fleur d'urbanité qui n'est point ailleurs.'

9. Although Mercier's first inclination was towards the Jacobin party, he refused to vote for the death of the King, and – in as far as he could ever be called a party man – he sided with the Girondins. He recorded his dislike of the Terror and the men who ran it, and he was imprisoned from October 1793 to December 1794: 'Dieu me préserve d'habiter jamais cette montagne, ou plutôt ce cratère sulfureux et fétide ou siègent des hommes de sang et de boue, des êtres stupides et féroces,' (quoted in H. Hofer, 'Situation de Mercier', p. 27, in *Louis-Sébastien Mercier*, ed. H. Hofer, Munich,

1977). The violence of the language is very typical of Mercier.

10. The most famous examples of great unfinished works of art are David's *Tennis-Court Oath* and Gérard's *10th of August 1792* (figs 21 and 37).

11. N. Hampson, *A Social History of the French Revolution*, London, 1963, p. 34.

12. P.-A. Caron de Beaumarchais, *La Folle Journée ou Le Mariage de Figaro*, Paris 1784, Act V, Sc. *iii*.

13. See A. Ribeiro, 'Fashion in the Eighteenth Century; Some Anglo-French Comparisons', in *Fabrics and Fashions: Studies in the Economic and Social History of Dress*, Pasold Studies in Textile History No. 9, ed. N. Harte, London 1989.

14. Rousseau's early beliefs led him to oppose the view taken by most of the contributors to the *Encyclopédie*, that the arts and sciences were vital in the fight for progress and the banishment of superstition; he felt that the arts in particular led to a corrupting sophistication inimical to a state of nature. However, in his most famous political work, the *Social Contract* (1762), he modified his views on the essential innocence of nature which, he accepted, could produce brutish beings, unthinking, and not always moral or virtuous; to be truly fulfilled and to contribute most to society, man must become a citizen.

15. George Rudé (in *Europe in the Eighteenth Century*, London, 1974, p. 211) notes that in 1779 there were 35 journals/newspapers, and in 1789 there were 169.

16. 'La Révolution française commença dans l'opinion publique du dix-huitième siècle; elle commença dans les salons,' was the opinion of the Goncourts in their *Histoire de la Société Française pendant la Révolution* (Paris, 1854, p. 1). Although the salons were not as important as they had been during the reign of Louis XV, they played a considerable part in the dissemination of new political ideas; they also inspired a number of provincial academies and literary societies, many of which became debating-grounds for politics.

17. Jean-Antoine Caritat, marquis de Condorcet (1743–94). Girondin member of the Legislative Assembly and the Convention; he committed suicide in prison during the Terror. His advocacy of political equality for women was tempered by the notion that the suffrage should be limited to women of property.

18. See J. Lough, 'Women in Mercier's Tableau de Paris', in *Woman and Society in Eighteenth-Century France: Essays in Honour of John Stephenson Spink*, ed. E. Jacobs and others, London 1979. In his blueprint for a perfect society, *L'An 2440* (1770), Mercier followed the Rousseau line in suggesting that women should look after the household and educate their children, rather than seek for intellectual pastimes. Yet in the *Tableau de Paris* he is sympathetic to the fact that women in some cases were being pushed by men out of jobs which had traditionally been theirs, such as hairdressers and 'marchandes de linge et des modes'. He is also quite modern in his approach to divorce, which he says should be allowed, even though he blames the breakdown in marriage very often on the wife's extravagance; divorce, introduced in 1792, was one of the few acts of the revolutionary government which genuinely improved the lot of women.

19. See Madame Campan's *Mémoires sur la vie privée de Marie-Antoinette, Reine de France*, Paris, 3 vols, 1822, I, p. 290. The spring toilettes served for autumn too. The official gowns were regarded as the perquisites of the queen's ladies and were rarely worn for more than a year, although Marie-Antoinette kept some which she particularly liked for longer. On average, the French queen ordered about 150 dresses a year, plus the other outfits (outer-wear and underwear) which a lady of fashion needed; even in the later 1780s when visible economies had to be made, she regularly overspent her allowance of 120,000 livres per year.

20. J. M. Roland de la Platière, *Encyclopédie Méthodique*, Paris 1785, I, p. 133.

21. M. de Valfons, *Souvenirs du Marquis de Valfons*, Paris 1860, p. 416.

22. See M. S. Boyce, 'The Barbier Manuscripts', in *Textile History*, vol. 12, 1981, pp. 52–3.

23. Chiné – textile designs produced by dyeing the warp threads before weaving.

24. See the *Livre-Journal de Madame Eloffe*, ed. G. A. H. de Reiset, Paris, 2 vols, 1885. Madame Eloffe was *couturière-lingère* to Marie-Antoinette, and her account book from 1787 to 1790 shows the popularity of chemise gowns with the royal ladies. Eloffe also supplied chemises to a range of wealthy and fashionable ladies.

25. Madame de Genlis describes the somewhat startling white and red complexion required for formal dress; rouge, in particular, was worn to excess in the evenings. See S. F. de Genlis, *Dictionnaire critique et raisonné des Étiquettes de la Cour et des Usages du Monde*, Paris, 2 vols, 1818, I, p. 79.

26. L. Fusil, *Souvenirs d'une Actrice*, Brussels, 2 vols, 1841, I, p. 105.

27. M. Rigoley de Juvigny, *De la Décadence des Lettres et des Moeurs Depuis les Grecs et les Romains jusqu' à nos Jours*, Paris 1787, p. 467.

28. See Rudé, op. cit., p. 191. He cites the English free press and the coffee houses where independent opinions could be discussed, and with regard to the arts, the realistic social commentary of the novel, and the work of Hogarth, 'whose refusal to come to terms with fashionable trends marked him off from all other artists of the time'.

29. After 1781, as part of the general decline in formality at Versailles, swords were worn only when taking leave of the King to return to one's regiment. See M. Delpierre, 'Marie-Antoinette, reine de la mode', in *Versailles*, No. 59, 1975, p. 38.

30. Mercier, op. cit., VII, p. 45.

31. F. d'Hézecques, *Souvenirs d'un Page de la Cour de Louis XVI*, ed. le comte d'Hézecques, Paris 1873, p. 190.

32. L. A. de Caraccioli, *Letters on the Manners of the French, and on the Follies and Extravagancies of the Times*, trans. C. Shillito, Dublin 1791, p. 128.

33. A. J. P. de Ségur, *Memoirs*, London, 3 vols, 1825–7, I, p. 21.

34. Mercier's comments on the details of English dress as translated into the wardrobe of the fashionable Frenchman are to be found throughout the *Tableau de Paris*, but especially VII, pp. 45–6.

35. Rigoley de Juvigny, op. cit., p. 465.

36. Mercier, op. cit., I, p. 144.

37. Quoted in A. Ribeiro, *Dress in Eighteenth Century Europe 1715–1789*, London 1984, p. 187.

2 Politics and Fashion 1789–1794

1. A. Young, *Travels during the Years 1787, 1788 and 1789*, London, 2nd ed. 1794, p. 137.

2. J. M. Thompson (ed.), *English Witnesses of the French Revolution*, Oxford 1938, p. 58.

3. Anon., *Lettre d'un Provincial, député aux États-Généraux sur le Costume de Cérémonie*, 1 May 1789, pp. 4–6.

4. *Ibid.*, p. 7. At least one of the deputies of the Third Estate chose to wear his own clothing and not the costume laid down by these regulations; Gouverneur Morris noted the cheers which greeted 'an old man who refused to dress in the costume prescribed for the Tiers, and who appears in his farmer's habit'. See *The Diary and Letters of Gouverneur Morris*, ed. A. C. Morris, London, 2 vols, 1889, I, p. 75.

5. In David's Versailles sketchbook (p. 64), he notes. '. . . beaucoup de gens font leurs serment avec les chapeaux qu'ils levent en l'air j'en ai vu le faire avec leurs chapeaux au bout de leurs cannes'. See V. Lee, 'Jacques-Louis David: the Versailles Sketchbook', in the *Burlington Magazine*, April and June 1969.

6. France was divided into 83 *départements*, although the number increased during the course of the revolutionary wars when further territory was annexed; by 1799 there were 90.

7. Active citizens paid taxes equal to three days' wages; they elected a board of electors who in turn elected the deputies. As well as participating in local and national elections and joining the National Guard, active citizens also elected the clergy.

   Passive citizens, who could not meet the tax qualifications, were excluded from the above.

8. The *Correspondence of William Augustus Miles on the French Revolution 1789–1817*, ed. C. P. Miles, London, 2 vols, 1890, I, p. 160.

9. *Ibid.*, I, p. 154.

10. *The Memoirs of François René, Vicomte de Chateaubriand*, ed. A. Teixeira de Mattos, London, 6 vols, 1902, I, p. 173.

11. Morris, op. cit., I, p. 252. The uniform of the National Guard in Paris consisted of a coat of royal blue with red collar and revers and gold buttons, white cloth breeches and hose and white gaiters; the officers added gold braid, epaulettes and a sword. Each district in Paris, however, seemed to have some slightly different interpretation of the uniform.

    Some fashionable young men wore other uniforms as part of the vogue for military costume. The *Journal de la Mode et du Goût* (15 March 1790) noted that the costume of the Chasseurs with its metal casque topped with a plume, its dark blue coat faced with white, blue pantaloons 'à la houzzarde' and black hussar buskins, was the glamorous choice of some young enthusiasts.

12. *Extracts of the Journals and Correspondence of Miss Berry 1783–1852*, ed. Lady Theresa Lewis, London, 3 vols, 1865, I, p. 218.

13. Thompson, op. cit, p. 94.

14. *Ibid.*, p. 96.

15. See A. Ribeiro, *Dress in Eighteenth Century Europe 1715–1789*, London 1984, pp. 138–9.

16. *Journal Général de la Cour et de la Ville*, 1 November 1789; such young men 'sont les débris de l'Aristocratie Françoise qui va périr au delà des mers . . .' (p. 352). It was rumours about this event that led to the march on Versailles by the women of Paris on 5 October.

17. Events in Paris at the time of the fall of the Bastille delayed the publication of the magazine; 'les circonstances trop fameuses & trop malheureuses où Paris s'est trouvé, nous ont empêché de le faire'.

18. *Livre-Journal de Madame Eloffe*, ed. G. A H. de Reiset, Paris, 2 vols, 1885, II, p. 87.

19. J. Hammond, *A Keeper of Royal Secrets, Being the Private and Political Life of Madame de Genlis*, London 1912, p. 191.

20. Chateaubriand, op. cit., II, p. 11.

21. The idea of 'right' and 'left' in politics came from the chance seating arrangements to the right or the left of the President's chair in the National Assembly.

22. *Madame Tussaud's Memoirs and Reminiscences of France*, ed. F. Hervé, London 1838, p. 177.

23. A. Jullien, *Histoire du Costume au Théâtre Depuis les Origines du Théâtre en France Jusqu' à nos Jours*, Paris 1880, p. 307. The *Journal de la Mode et du Goût* (15 November 1790) had already noted that the vogue for simplicity in dress had caused men to have their hair 'coupés et frisés comme ceux d'une tête antique'.

24. J. Moore, *A Journal during a residence in France from the beginning of August to the middle of December 1792*, London, 2 vols, 1793, II, p. 430.

25. H. M. Williams, *Letters from France*, ed. & intr. J. M. Todd, New York, 2 vols, 1975, II, p. 193. The word *muscadin(e)* was used, during the Terror, and for some time afterwards, to indicate any counter–revolutionary activity.

26. *Ibid.*, I, p. 194.

27. Tussaud, op. cit., p. 254. The author states that she took a number of casts (from life, and after death) of some of the main figures in the Revolution. Robespierre's cast was taken on his death (p. 254), but Madame Tussaud records later (p. 425) that she had already taken a cast from life; he sent her his own clothes so that the figure could be properly dressed, and he stated that he wished it to be placed next to Marat in the waxworks museum.

28. From the *Correspondance politique* (10 Floréal, An II), quoted in G. Walter, *La Révolution française vue par ses journaux*, Paris, 1948, p. 410.

29. P. de Nouvion, *Un ministre des modes sous Louis XVI: Mademoiselle Bertin, Marchande de Modes de la Reine 1747–1813*, Paris 1911, p. 99. Most of the money spent in 1792 appears to have been on alterations.

    The allowance for clothing, although considerably reduced, was still substantial in terms of money values. In 1789, 24 livres (a louis d'or) was worth £1; an écu of 6 livres was worth 5/-.

30. F. d'Hézecques, *Souvenirs d'un Page de la Cour de Louis XVI*, Paris 1873, p. 15. Court pages were abolished on 1 January 1790, and d'Hézecques became an equerry; he emigrated in April 1791.

31. J. G. Millingen, *Recollections of Republican France from 1790 to 1801*, London 1848, p. 120. Millingen, son of a republican Dutch father who looked on France as 'an El Dorado of freedom' and who had moved his family to Paris in 1790, was born in 1782. He was only a child during the Revolution, but there is no reason to believe that his recollections are less accurate than any other memoirs coloured by bias and the passage of time. Millingen was old enough to be aware of household tensions (his mother was a monarchist) and, maybe for this reason, he wandered the streets of Paris during the Terror, and during the years that followed it.

32. Nouvion, op. cit., p. 164. In 1795 her name was removed from the list of *émigrés*, and in 1800 she was finally granted the right to live in France.

33. *A Journal of the Terror, Being an account of the occurrences in the Temple during the Confinement of Louis XVI, by M. Cléry, the King's valet-de-chambre ...*, London 1798, ed. S. Scott, London 1955, p. 42.

34. E. Langlade, *Rose Bertin: The Creator of Fashion at the Court of Marie-Antoinette*, trans. & adapted A. S. Rappoport, London 1913, p. 233.

35. On the conditions in prison, see O. Blanc, *Last Letters: Prisons and Prisoners of the French Revolution*, trans. A. Sheridan, London 1987.

36. *Life and Adventures of Count Beugnot*, ed. C. M. Yonge, London, 2 vols, 1871, I, p. 179.

37. Morris, op. cit., I, p. 368.

38. See R. Twiss, *A Trip to Paris in July and August 1792*, Dublin 1793, p. 72. Richard Twiss found in the cafés of Paris that the chess pieces all looked alike, and there was some discussion about abolishing such names as king, queen, knight and bishop.

    In April 1794 the nobility were forbidden to reside in Paris.

39. Beugnot, op. cit., I, p. 179. *Blonde* is silk lace. Madame Roland was guillotined in November 1793.

40. S. Loomis, *Paris in the Terror*, Philadelphia 1964, p. 125.

41. M. S. Boyce, 'The Barbier Manuscripts', in *Textile History*, vol. 12, 1981, p. 53. Late in 1793 we find the first use of the terms 'citoyen/citoyenne' occurring in Barbier's business correspondence.

42. G. Duval, *Souvenirs Thermidoriens*, Paris, 2 vols, 1844, I, p. 53. The cockade had to be quite large to

escape public comment, and entry to public gardens was refused 'à toute femme non cocardée'.

43. Millingen, op. cit., p. 217. Mercier, however, in the *Nouveau Paris*, did not remember such a vogue in Paris, although he saw, in Nantes, women wearing enamel jewellery in the shape of the guillotine.

Since women's valuable jewellery had been given either freely or under compulsion to the government (Dr Moore noted in the autumn of 1792 that rings and bracelets were taken from women in the streets of Paris, ostensibly for the war effort), they were left with obviously non-precious materials, like copper (particularly used for buckles) and pinchbeck, a zinc and copper alloy.

44. Morris, op. cit., I, p. 368.

45. *Journal de la Mode et du Goût*, 1 April 1792, pp. 3–4.

46. *Journal de Paris*, 19 October 1793, pp. 1–2. Mme Raspal offered a postal service or a personal service, and gave a reduction to those who brought with them their own lining materials.

47. Duval, op. cit., I, p. 53. Williams also says (*Letters*, II, p. 193) that hats were frowned upon as a sign of a 'muscadine'. More acceptable, because less formal and simpler in style, was the bonnet, which had more crown than brim, and usually tied under the chin.

48. *Memoirs of the Duchess d'Abrantès*, London, 8 vols, 1831–5, I, p. 112.

49. *Journal de Paris*, 31 October 1794, pp. 1–3, as 'Lisfrand jadis Teillard'. The business (I have first seen it advertised in the *Journal de Paris* in October 1790) survived into the Directory.

3 Brave New World: People and State 1789–1795

1. 'On 23 August (1793) the Convention agreed in principle to mobilize the nation for war by ordering a *levée en masse* of the whole French population: while the young should go to battle and married men forge arms, women stitch tents and uniforms and children make bandages, even the old men were to "repair to the public places, stimulate the courage of the warriors and preach the unity of the Republic and the hatred of Kings".' (G. Rudé, *Revolutionary Europe 1783–1815*, London 1964, p. 145.) Olwen Hufton notes ('Women in Revolution 1789–1796', in *Past and Present*, Oxford 1971, p. 100) that many women sacrificed their precious dowries of linen to make bandages for the troops.

2. Divorce was abolished in 1816 and not restored until 1884.

3. In 1795 a decimal coinage based on the franc was instituted, replacing the livre, although the latter continued to be widely used until the end of the century. In 1803 by a law of 17 Germinal (7 April) a louis d'or (worth 24 livres in 1789) became a 20 franc piece or gold napoléon; a silver écu (worth 6 livres in 1789) became a 5 franc piece.

4. C. C. Brinton, *The Jacobins*, New York 1930, p. 18.

5. *Ibid.*, p. 39. In the summer of 1792 Richard Twiss was told that there were about 1300 members in Paris.

6. Anatole France, *Les Opinions de M. Jérôme Coignard*, 1893, pp. 25–6.

7. A.-E. Gibelin, *De l'Origine et de la Forme du Bonnet de la Liberté*, Paris 1796, p. 16 *et seq*. He is emphatic about the fact that the *bonnet rouge* is *not* the Phrygian cap, which came from Asia, but a semi-oval shape, loose and elongated with the top falling down at the front or the back – a type with Roman origins.

In the Middle Ages a similarly shaped cap was worn to celebrate the end of apprenticeship, and by the sixteenth century there are a few references to it as a general item of working class/peasant dress in France.

Although in the eighteenth century the *bonnet rouge* was usually identified with ideals of freedom (it can be seen in a number of history paintings), to Mercier, having lived through the Revolution, it was 'the signal of anarchy'; it was in the latter sense that Hogarth, in his famous engraving, had depicted John Wilkes in 1763 as an ugly demagogue with a cap of liberty on a pole.

A number of *bonnets rouges* survive in museum collections, for example the Musée Carnavalet, Paris, the Musée Historique des Tissus, Lyon, and the Museum of Fine Arts, Boston.

8. The red flag was first seen in the massacre of the Champ de Mars on 17 July 1791, used by the authorities as a sign that they might fire on the crowd if they didn't disperse; it was taken over by the revolutionaries as a sign of the 'Martial Law of the Sovereign People'.

 With a great deal of hindsight, J. Grasset de Saint-Sauveur in his *L' Esprit des Ana* (1801) says that the colour red: 'annonce ambition bien-marquée, le non-repos, le trouble, l'esprit de révolution, les combats, les massacres et l'insensibilité' (II, p. 165).

9. *The Memoirs of François René, Vicomte de Chateaubriand*, ed. A. Teixeira de Mattos, London, 6 vols, 1902, II, p. 15.

10. A. Soboul, *The Parisian Sans-Culottes and the French Revolution 1793–4*, trans. G. Lewis, Oxford 1964, p. 223.

11. G. Walter, *La Révolution française vue par ses journaux*, Paris 1948, p. 384.

12. R. Twiss, *A Trip to Paris in July and August 1792*, Dublin 1793, p. 105.

13. J. Harris, *The Red Cap of Liberty*, in *Eighteenth-Century Studies*, Spring 1981, p. 292.

14. Gibelin, op. cit., pp. 5–6.

15. J. Moore, *A Journal during a residence in France from the beginning of August to the middle of December 1792*, London, 2 vols, 1793, I, p. 197.

16. L.-S. Mercier, *Le Nouveau Paris*, Paris, 6 vols, 1798, III, p. 204.

17. Twiss, op. cit., p. 137.

18. C. C. Brinton, *A Decade of Revolution 1789–1799*, New York 1934, p. 144.

19. In the spring of 1790 Paris was divided, for political and electoral purposes, into 48 *sections*; they became important debating assemblies, they petitioned national government, and they also acted as military units. The names of the most militant sections testified to their revolutionary zeal; they included the 'Bonnet-Rouge ou de la Liberté . . . des Droits de l'Homme, auparavant du Roi-de-Sicile . . . de la Fraternité, dite aussi de l'Ile Saint-Louis, . . . du Jardin des Plantes ou des Sans-Culottes . . .' etc. (Décembre-Alonnier, *Dictionnaire de la Révolution française*, II, pp. 508–9).

20. Such deputations were often laughed at because they wore their own hair (instead of a wig) and no buckles to their shoes; the Girondin minister, Roland, was at first refused admittance by the Master of Ceremonies because he wore no buckles. See H. M. Williams, *Letters from France*, I, p. 81.

21. *Madame Tussaud's Memoirs and Reminiscences of France*, ed. F. Hervé, London 1838, p. 196.

22. M. Beauvert, *Caricatures Politiques*, Paris, An VI, pp. 7–8.

23. Williams, op. cit., II, p. 193.

24. Soboul, op. cit., p. 244.

25. J. Michelet, *Les Femmes de la Révolution*, Paris 1857, p. 26.

26. The word itself was not coined until 1837 by Charles Fourier.

27. J. G. Millingen, *Recollections of Republican France from 1790 to 1801*, London 1848, p. 123. Moore (op. cit., I, p. 117) saw her 'dressed in a kind of English riding habit, but her jacket was the uniform of the national guards'.

28. This is article X of her *Déclaration des Droits de la Femme*, 1791. A useful discussion of her life and work can be found in Olivier Blanc's *Olympe de Gouges*, Paris 1981.

29. Millingen, op. cit., p. 244.

30. H. B. Applewhite, M. D. Johnson & D. G. Levy, *Women in Revolutionary Paris 1789–1795*, Chicago 1979, p. 213. The society met in the former church of Saint-Eustache in Les Halles; following the example set by the masculine revolutionary clubs, the president (a new one was chosen every month) wore the cap of liberty.

31. Applewhite, op. cit., p. 5. The market women also wanted the Convention to abolish the *Société des Républicaines-Révolutionnaires* because the SRR wanted price controls which the market women feared would lead to a loss in income.

32. Already by the summer of 1792, Richard Twiss found the *sans-culottes* talking of pulling down all the theatres because they corrupted the morals of the people.

 It was difficult to know if it was safer to stay indoors, or to be outside demonstrating loyalty to the new regime; in either case you could be spied on by unfriendly neighbours and denounced for being, if not an aristocrat, then a *modéré*. Private hatreds could easily assume the more virtuous mantle of political differences, and informing the authorities of any transgression became a 'public duty'.

33. See O. Hufton, 'Women in Revolution 1789–1796', in *Past and Present*, Oxford 1971.

34. O. Hufton, *The Poor of Eighteenth-Century France 1750–1789*, Oxford, 1974, p. 259.

35. R. Cobb, *Death in Paris 1795–1801*, Oxford 1978. This detailed study (covering the Directory and the early years of the Consulate) is based on the records of the Basse-Geôle de la Seine from October 1795 to September 1801.

36. Twiss, op. cit., pp. 83–4. Such women were probably of a slightly higher class than the ones described by Cobb; in the latter case the costume of the poor women committing suicide consisted, in the main, of a *casaquin* (tight-fitting jacket) and skirt. Twiss's 'white linen or muslin gowns' would be the likely wear of personal maids or girls working in fashion shops.

37. Walter, op. cit., p. 394. The quotation is from *La Feuille villageoise* of 19 April 1792.

38. Twiss, op. cit., p. 13.

39. A. Mathiez, *Les Origines des Cultes Révolutionnaires 1789–1792*, Paris 1904, p. 31. Such altars lasted until the first days of the Empire.

40. Archives Nationales, *Comité de Salut Public: Esprit Public, Arts, Caricatures, Costume national*, AF II 484, f. 38. Although it is hard to define precisely what Robespierre's religious beliefs were (they seem to be just as vague as Mercier's in *L'An 2440* not altogether surprisingly as both men were disciples of Rousseau), they were strongly held. In the spring of 1794 he sent to the guillotine the *Enragés* and the *Hébertistes* (both extreme republican groups) for their advocacy of anarchy and atheism.

41. Millingen, op. cit., p. 276. See also C.S.P. AF II 489, f. 14.

42. There is little agreement as to what kind of woman took the role of the Goddess of Reason. Mercier says she was usually a girl from the *sans-culottes*, Millingen notes that in his *section* she was an 'opera-dancer' (certainly in Notre Dame it was an actress), but Michelet, whole-hearted in his enthusiasm for the Revolution, counters the frequent accusations of the goddesses' immorality by

stating firmly that nearly always it was 'une femme sérieuse et d'une vie toujours exemplaire'.

43. Twiss, op. cit., pp. 17 and 14.

44. Mercier, op. cit., IV, pp. 132–7.

45. *The Times* (20 June 1794), in its account of the event, noted that each Paris *section* elected 10 old men, 10 matrons, 10 young girls, 10 youths, and 10 male infants (under eight years of age) to sit on the mountain. Citizens were urged to decorate their houses with 'the cherished colours of liberty'. The festival was copied all over France, in the French colonies and also imitated in America – see D. L. Dowd, *Pageant-Master of the Republic: Jacques-Louis David and the French Revolution*, Lincoln, Nebraska 1948, p. 126.

46. Williams, op. cit., I, p. 22.

47. H. T. Parker, *The Cult of Antiquity and the French Revolution*, Chicago 1937, p. 39.

48. L. Fusil, *Souvenirs d'une Actrice*, Brussels, 2 vols, 1841, II, p. 96.

49. At his death, Saint-Just was planning a kind of Spartan national militia; selected boys (aged 5 to 16) were to be raised by the state, dressed in linen all the year round to make them hardy, and to have a largely vegetarian diet.

50. Parker, op. cit., p. 147

51. *Aux Armes et aux Arts: Journal de la Société Républicaine des Arts*, vol. 1, Feb.–May 1794, p. 199.

52. D. L. Dowd, *Pageant-Master of the Republic: Jacques-Louis David and the French Revolution*, Lincoln, Nebraska 1948, p. 82. Dowd's is still the most comprehensive source in English for the festivals designed by David.

53. *Ibid.*, p. 60.

54. *Ibid.*, p. 112.

55. See M. Carlson, *The Theatre of the French Revolution*, New York 1966.

56. A. Jullien, *Histoire du Costume au Théâtre Depuis les Origines du Théâtre en France Jusqu' à nos Jours*, Paris 1880, p. 293.

57. Useful contemporary sources for historical accuracy in stage costume were J. C. Le Vacher de Charnois's *Costumes et annales des grands théâtres de Paris*, 1787–9 (Talma had a copy), and his *Recherches sur les costumes et sur les théâtres de toutes les nations*, 1790.

58. *Souvenirs of Madame Vigée Le Brun*, London, 2 vols, 1879, I, p. 88 *et seq*. Vigée Le Brun particularly admired David's teacher Joseph-Marie Vien, as the first artist who 'rendered Greek and Roman dress in style and accuracy'.

59. Harris, op. cit., p. 293.

60. Louise Fusil, however, (I, p. 148) says that for the *Fête de la Fédération*, she and a number of other actresses thought white was too impractical and wore grey muslin, with a straw hat and a tricolour sash.

61. The dramatic horror of the death of Marat, one of the great heroes of the people, inspired a play performed in August (*L'Ami du peuple, ou La Mort de Marat*); and at the waxworks museum 'a representation was exhibited of Marat's assassination which attracted huge crowds', including Robespierre. See Tussaud, op. cit., p. 345.

On the other side of the chair of the President of the National Convention was a painting by David of another 'martyr', the deputy Michael Le Pelletier de Saint-Fargeau, who had been murdered by the royal bodyguard in January 1793 for voting for the death of the King. David organized his state funeral, during which his bloodstained clothing was carried on a pike. The painting (presumed destroyed) is now known only as a mutilated engraving and a drawing after the original.

62. All belonging to this society had to affirm allegiance to the republican constitution; artists whose enthusiasm was less than whole-hearted, were denounced. A Committee of Public Instruction was set up (David was on it) to teach people about the role of art in a republic. A Jury of the Arts was intended to commission republican works of art glorifying the ideas and events of the French Revolution, but very little was produced; many artists were reluctant to become too politically involved and there was bound to be tension between republican ideology and artistic freedom. See J. A. Leith, *The Idea of Art as Propaganda in France 1750–1799*, Toronto 1965.

63. During the Thermidorean Reaction (and indeed during the Directory) there was no longer that total harmony of state, politics and theatre which was necessary to create the most successful propaganda. Such fêtes cost thousands of livres, and required an army of painters, carpenters and tailors to make the painted backdrops, the triumphal arches, the 'statues' and 'mountains', the banners and the costumes. After the fall of Robespierre, the new government was not only opposed to Jacobin ideology, but reluctant to spend vast sums of money on festivals when the money could be used for the war effort.

64. Moore, op. cit., II, p. 433.

65. However the military Order of St Louis was allowed to continue until 1793 when it was abolished by the Convention.

66. Soboul, op. cit., p. 230. Twiss (op. cit., p. 131) says that the *sans-culottes* wanted army officers to wear 'worstead instead of gold or silver shoulder-knots'.

67. One of the first acts of the wise foreign visitor to France was to buy himself a cockade, otherwise he might be subject to insults. When in July 1792 Richard Twiss landed at Calais, he immediately 'procured a national cockade, which was a silk ribband, with blue, white and red stripes' (Twiss, op. cit., p. 4).

68. *Aux Armes et aux Arts*, op. cit., pp. 315–16.

69. The author writes in the *Décade philosophique et littéraire*, published by 'une société de républicains' in Fructidor, An II; it is quoted in J. Renouvier, *Histoire de l'Art pendant la Révolution*, Paris 1863, p. 472.

70. Renouvier, op. cit., p. 416.

71. *Aux Armes et aux Arts*, op. cit., p. 258. It is impossible to know how many artists submitted designs. The Carnavalet museum, for example, has three designs attributed to Pierre Etienne Le Sueur, which may be by him, or copied from the designs of other artists. Le Sueur was a member of the Société Populaire et Republicaine des Arts. See M. Delpierre, *A propos d'un manteau de représentant du peuple de 1798 récemment offert au Musée du Costume*, in the *Bulletin du Musée Carnavalet* 1972, No. 1.

72. C.S.P., op. cit. AF II 489, f. 15.

73. The original designs are as follows:
le citoyen français
le citoyen français dans l'intérieur
le représentant du peuple
le représentant du peuple aux armées
le législateur en fonctions

l'officier municipal
le juge

74. Millingen, op. cit., p. 311.

75. W. Hooper, *Memoirs of the Year Two Thousand Five Hundred*, London, 2 vols, 1772, I, p. 22. This is an English translation of Mercier's book, the title presumably being altered for reasons of symmetry. The original work was published anonymously in 1770 in Amsterdam, as it was thought too fierce a satire on the French government. Mercier acknowledged his authorship only in 1799.

In 2440, according to Mercier, France still has a king, although he is a citizen-ruler, who lives in Paris and goes everywhere on foot. Although there is still an aristocracy, honour is attached to personal merit, and such citizens are rewarded by the king by being authorized to wear their names in their hats. Both the king, and a senate (which holds the executive power) are responsible to a legislative assembly elected every two years. The law has been reformed, reason guides religion, and the Supreme Being is worshipped in the Temple of God.

Mercier, while acknowledging his debt to Rousseau, rightly claimed (in the preface to the third edition of *L'An 2440*, 1799) that he had anticipated many of the events of the French Revolution.

76. C.S.P. op. cit., AF II 489, f. 19. David was instructed by the Committee of Public Safety to have engraved 6000 copies of each of the designs for the legislature and the military, and 20,000 of the civilian designs.

The Archives Nationales (*Comité de Salut Public: Esprit public, Arts, Caricatures, Costume national, AF II 489*) contains the documents ordering David's costume designs, his expenses, the arrangements for the engravings, etc.; seven of Vivant-Denon's engravings are also there – the one of the judge is missing.

77. A. V. Arnault, *Souvenirs d'un Sexagénaire*, Paris, 4 vols, 1833, III, p. 369.

78. *Memoirs of the Duchess d'Abrantès*, London, 8 vols, 1831–5, I, p. 276. She notes that there were about 200–300 young men dressed in this way. It is not clear if she is describing the costume to which Millingen (op. cit., p. 110) sarcastically refers:

'Several of David's pupils, in imitation of their master's love of antiquity, had formed themselves into a society called Les Penseurs. They wore a Phrygian costume, and used to assemble and remain for a long time in silent cogitation, until one of them spoke, and delivered his opinion on Grecian perfection.' By 'Phrygian costume', Millingen might mean a Greek *chiton* or tunic. The duchess, although she talks about a toga – a garment only worn in ancient Rome – goes on to describe the 'artists and literary men . . . dressed completely in the Grecian style'.

79. *Rapport et projet de décret présentés au nom du Comité d'instruction publique, sur les costumes des législateurs et des autres fonctionnaires publics. Séance du 28 Fructidor an III (14 Sept. 1795) par Grégoire, député à la Convention Paris 6 complémentaire an III (22 Sept. 1795).*

80. J. Grasset de Saint-Sauveur, *Costumes des Représentans du Peuple Français*, Paris 1795, p. 4. The designs were engraved by 'Citoyen Labrousse, artiste de Bordeaux'. Grasset de Saint-Sauveur was the author of a number of books on costume. He was particularly interested in the costume of the ancient world, and in 1796 published *L'Antique Rome*.

81. d'Abrantès, op. cit., I, p. 263.

82. *Moniteur* (29 Brumaire An VI–19 Nov. 1797), quoted in Delpierre, op. cit., p. 16.

83. F. W. Blagdon, *Paris as it was and as it is*, London, 2 vols, 1803, II, p. 245. The uniformity consisted in the fact that the legislators wore blue coats, with silver embroidery for the members of the *Tribune* (this, like the old *Council of 500*, proposed laws), and gold embroidery for the *Legislative Council* (which, like the *Council of Ancients*, passed them); the tricolour sash was also worn.

For the details of official dress in the Directory and in the Consulate, see Delpierre (op. cit.), and the exhibition catalogue *Uniformes Civils français Cérémonial Circonstances 1750–1950*, Musée de la Mode et du Costume, Paris 1982–3.

84. The most detailed examination of the elaborate system of court and official dress under Napoleon, is in M. Delpierre, 'Les costumes de cour et les uniformes civils du Premier Empire', in the *Bulletin du Musée Carnavalet*, 1958, No. 2.

4 Decline and Fall: Thermidor and Directory 1794–1799

1. M. Lyons, *France under the Directory*, Cambridge 1975, p. 113. He notes that in 1800 non-juring priests were set free, and estimates that about 55% had previously taken the oath. Any lingering form of civic religion ended when the Concordat was signed with the Papacy in 1801.

2. These were the four main festivals – 14 July, 10 August, 21 January, and 31 May; in addition, a fête was held to celebrate the birth of the republic (1 Vendémiaire), from 1796 to 1801. There were also occasional celebrations of such themes as 'youth', 'nature', 'agriculture' etc., initiated by the Jacobin regime and carried on into the Directory.

3. P. Lacroix, *Directoire, Consulat et Empire*, Paris 1884, p. 196.

4. *Memoirs of Count Miot de Melito*, ed. General Fleischmann, London, 2 volumes, 1881, I, p. 262.

5. *Ibid.*

6. It had become a well-known haunt of prostitutes. During the Terror, prostitution was banned, denounced as a part of the libertine manners and decadence associated with the aristocracy. However, a few days after the fall of Robespierre, prostitutes appeared again in the Palais-Egalité.

7. *Tableau Général du Goût, des Modes et Costumes de Paris*, Paris, 2 vols, 1797–9, I, p. 58.

8. M. Beauvert, *Caricatures Politiques*, Paris An VI (1797–8), pp. 13–16, 10–12.

9. *Ibid.*, pp. 4–6.

10. *Ibid.*, pp. 7–8. Mercier in his *Le Nouveau Paris* (IV pp. 254–5) has a symbolic description of *l'exclusif*, standing in the attitude of a gladiator, his eyes sparkling with fury and his pockets full of denunciations; a pistol in one hand is labelled 'death', a dagger in the other is named 'fraternity'; he has a cap of liberty on his head, and 'un petit bonnet rouge est pendu à son boutonnière'.

11. Beauvert, op. cit., p. 17.

12. *Conseils aux sans-culottes*, anon., no date and no pagination (British Library). Another popular song, *Les Sans-Culottes*, extolled the virtues of trousers, which it urged their wearers not to give up. See C. A. Dauban, *Paris en 1794 et en 1795*, Paris 1869, p. 539.

13. Richard Cobb, in his study of the clothing of the suicides of Paris (*Death in Paris 1795–1801*, Oxford 1978) notes that in spite of the law enforcing the wearing of cockades, none were listed in the effects of the dead.

Does this indicate that the cockade was so treasured that it was removed before its wearer committed suicide? Or (and this seems more likely) that it was only worn by the politically active; men and women who had a stake in society?

Foreigners, being more identifiable objects of suspicion, were made to wear the cockade. In October 1796, the Earl of Malmesbury came to Paris to negotiate with the French government; he found the wearing of the national cockade 'universal in the streets, and ... unpleasantly enforced by the populace'. (*Diaries and Correspondence of James Harris, First Earl of Malmesbury*, ed. 3rd Earl of Malmesbury, London, 4 vols, 1844, III, p. 269.)

By the time of the Consulate the wearing of the cockade seems to have been on the decline. English visitors to France during the Peace of Amiens (1802–3) noted that it continued to be worn by the military, but not by many civilians.

14. G. Duval, *Souvenirs Thermidoriens*, Paris, 2 vols, 1844, II, p. 298.

15. *Ibid.*, II, p. 10.

16. *Memoirs of the Duchess d'Abrantès*, London, 8 vols, 1831–5, I, p. 115.

17. F. Gendron, *La Jeunesse dorée*, Quebec, 1979, p. 33. *Chouans* were counter-revolutionary peasant guerrillas operating in Brittany and Normandy after 1793.

18. L.-S. Mercier, *Le Nouveau Paris*, Paris, 6 vols, 1798, IV, p. 49.

19. S. Mercier, *New Picture of Paris*, Dublin, 2 vols, 1800, II, p. 163. In September 1797 the *Journal des Dames et des Modes* records the reappearance of shoe buckles, in abeyance during the Revolution.

20. *Tableau Général*, op. cit., I, p. 12.

21. *Ibid.*, II, p. 193.

22. Abroad, it was often equated with Jacobinism. Among the French fashions proscribed in Milan in 1799, according to *L'Ami des Lois*, were hair 'à la Titus', round hats, and 'cravates larges et

bouffantes'. See A. Aulard, *Paris pendant la Réaction Thermidorienne et sous le Directoire*, Paris, 5 vols, 1898–1902, V, p. 586.

23. J. C. Flügel, *The Psychology of Clothes*, London 1930.

24. E. & J. de Goncourt, *Histoire de la Société Française pendant le Directoire*, Paris 1855, p. 139.

25. Lacroix, op. cit., p. 28.

26. Duval, op. cit., II, p. 81. Charles-Henri Sanson was the public executioner.

27. There was also a greeting *à la victime*, a ducking motion which imitated the movement of the head being inserted in the lunette of the guillotine.

28. *Journal des Dames et des Modes*, 30 Floréal (19 May) 1798, pp. 8–9.

29. *New Picture of Paris*, op. cit., I, p. 181.

30. Mercier, op. cit., III, p. 136.

31. See the *Journal des Dames et des Modes*, 9 Pluviôse (28 January) 1798. Madame Tallien, it is reported, favoured flesh-coloured tights spangled with gold, which glittered under a diaphanous robe.

32. d'Abrantès, op. cit., I, p. 247.

33. *Tableau Général*, op. cit., II, pp. 166–7.

34. L. Fusil, *Souvenirs d'une Actrice*, Brussels, 2 vols, 1841, II, p. 100.

35. *Journal des Dames et des Modes*, 20 Germinal (9 April) 1799. It was called (until 16 September 1797) the *Journal des Modes et des Nouveautés*. The editor was Pierre la Mésangère, a former Oratorian priest and professor of philosophy. Lyons (op. cit., p. 142) remarks that in terms of circulation, it was 'the most successful fashion paper of the Directory'.

36. Fusil, op. cit., p. 100.

37. A. V. Arnault, *Souvenirs d'un Sexagénaire*, Paris, 4 vols, 1833, II, p. 313.

38. d'Abrantès, op. cit., IV, p. 51.

39. *New Picture of Paris*, op. cit., II, p. 163.

40. *Feuilleton de Littérature, Spectacles, Anecdotes, Modes et Avis Divers*, Paris, 18 Thermidor (5 August) 1797.

41. With the nationalization of Church property in 1790, a commission was set up to choose works of art for the nation from the confiscated possessions of the Church. This collection (which opened to the public as the *Musée des Monuments Français* in

1795) was a particular haunt of those artists who wished to study the medieval and Renaissance art objects – stained glass, sculpture etc. – on display.

42. M. R. Mitford, *Our Village: Sketches of Rural Scenery*, London, 5 vols, 1824–32, II, p. 213. The reference is to the French *émigrées* whom Mary Russell Mitford remembered from her youth.

43. Mercier, op. cit., IV, pp. 68–70.

44. Quoted in E. J. Knapton, *Empress Josephine*, London 1969, p. 140. It was rumoured that during the Terror some women had worn wigs made from the hair of guillotined blondes; see Mercier's *Nouveau Tableau*, II, p. 134.

45. Mercier, op. cit., III, p. 181.

46. Aulard, op. cit., II, P. 630.

47. Mercier, op. cit., III, p. 28.

48. Aulard, op. cit., IV, p. 139.

49. Aulard, op. cit., IV, p. 312.

5 Postcript

1. *Madame Tussaud's Memoirs and Reminiscences of France*, ed. F. Hervé, London 1838, p. 491.

2. *Memoirs of Count Miot de Melito*, ed. General Fleischmann, London, 2 vols, 1881, I, p. 305.

3. L.-S. Mercier, *Le Nouveau Paris*, Paris, 6 vols, 1798, p. 208, where Napoleon's appearance is also described in lyrical terms.

4. *Memoirs of the Duchess d'Abrantès*, London, 8 vols, 1831–5, I, p. 114 & 143.

5. *Memoirs of Madame de Rémusat*, ed. P. de Rémusat, trans. C. Hoey & J. Lillie, London, 2 vols, 1880, I, p. 71.

6. W. Geer, *Napoleon and Josephine*, New York, 1924, p. 94.

7. *Miot de Melito*, op. cit., p. 49.

8. As Emperor, Napoleon's preferred dress was uniform, that of Colonel of the *Chasseurs à Cheval de la Garde* (green with red facings) on weekdays, and that of Colonel of the *Grenadiers à Pied de la Garde* (blue faced with white) on Sundays.

9. See M. Delpierre, 'Les costumes de cour et les uniformes civils du Premier Empire', in the *Bulletin du Musée Carnavalet*, 1958, No. 2.

APPENDIX
The Revolutionary Calendar

This was established in October 1793, the first year being regarded retrospectively as beginning on 22 September 1792, the day after the abolition of the monarchy. The year was divided up into ten months named after the climate of Paris and its vicinity. Each month consisted of three *décades* of ten days each, each tenth day (*décadi*) being a holiday; at the end of the year there were added five extra days, *jours complémentaires*, also called *jours sans-culottides*. The calendar was in force until 1 January 1806.

Years

An II	22 September 1793–21 September 1794
An III	22 September 1794–21 September 1795
An IV	22 September 1795–21 September 1796
An V	22 September 1796–21 September 1797
An VI	22 September 1797–21 September 1798
An VII	22 September 1798–21 September 1799
An VIII	22 September 1799–21 September 1800

The months

Vendémiare (vintage)	22 September–21 October
Brumaire (fog)	22 October–20 November
Frimaire (frost)	21 November–20 December
Nivôse (snow)	21 December–19 January
Pluviôse (rain)	20 January–18 February
Ventôse (wind)	19 February–20 March
Germinal (budding)	21 March–19 April
Floréal (flowers)	20 April–19 May
Prairial (meadows)	20 May–18 June
Messidor (harvest)	19 June–18 July
Thermidor (heat)	19 July–17 August
Fructidor (fruit)	18 August–16 September
Sans-culottides	17–21 September

Select bibliography

Note: From the vast literature on the French Revolution, I have the space here to list only a small selection of the works which – as a historian of society and of dress – I found useful. Readers should refer to the notes to the text for further references.

Books

Applewhite, H. B., Johnson, M. D. & Levy, D. G., *Women in Revolutionary Paris 1789–1795*, Chicago 1979

Aulard, A., *Paris pendant le Réaction Thermidorienne et sous le Directoire*, Paris, 5 vols, 1898–1902

Beclard, L., *Sébastien Mercier, Sa Vie, Son Oeuvre, Son Temps*, Paris 1903

Biver, M.-L., *Fêtes révolutionnaires à Paris*, Paris 1979

Braudel, F., *Civilization and Capitalism 15th to 18th Century*, London, 3 vols, 1981

Brinton, C. C., *The Jacobins*, New York 1930

— *A Decade of Revolution 1789–1799*, New York 1934

Brookner, A., *Jacques-Louis David*, London 1980

Carlson, M., *The Theatre of the French Revolution*, New York 1966

Cobb, R., *The Police and the People: French Popular Protest 1789–1820*, Oxford 1970

— *Death in Paris 1795–1801*, Oxford 1978

Décembre, J. & Alonnier, E., *Dictionnaire de la Révolution française 1789–1799*, Paris, 2 vols 1866–8

Dowd, D. L., *Pageant-Master of the Republic: Jacques-Louis David and the French Revolution*, Lincoln, Nebraska 1948

Fusil, L., *Souvenirs d'une Actrice*, Brussels, 2 vols, 1841

Gaxotte, P., *Paris au XVIIIᵉ siècle*, Paris 1982

Gendron, F., *La Jeunesse dorée: Episodes de la Révolution française*, Quebec 1979

Goncourt, E. & J. de, *Histoire de la Société Française pendant la Révolution*, Paris 1854

— *Histoire de la Société Française pendant le Directoire*, Paris 1855

Hampson, N., *A Social History of the French Revolution*, London 1963

— *Will and Circumstance*, London 1983

Hobsbawm, E. J., *The Age of Revolution 1789–1848*, London 1962

Lacroix, P., *Directoire, Consulat et Empire: Moeurs et Usages, Lettres, Sciences et Arts 1795–1815*, Paris 1884

Lee, V., *The Reign of Women in Eighteenth-Century France*, Cambridge Mass. 1975

Leith, J. A., *The Idea of Art as Propaganda in France 1750–1799*, Toronto 1965

Lyons, M., *France under the Directory*, Cambridge 1975

Mathiez, A., *Les Origines des Cultes Révolutionnaires 1789–1792*, Paris 1904

Mercier, L.-S., *Tableau de Paris*, Amsterdam, 8 vols, 1782–8

— *Le Nouveau Paris*, Paris, 6 vols, 1798

Millingen, J. G., *Recollections of Republican France From 1790 to 1801*, London 1848

Moore, J., *A Journal during a residence in France from the beginning of August to the middle of December 1792*, London, 2 vols, 1793

Parker, H. T., *The Cult of Antiquity and the French Revolution*, Chicago 1937

R. Paulson, *Representations of Revolution 1789–1820*, New Haven & London 1983

Renouvier, J., *Histoire de l'Art pendant la Révolution*, Paris 1863

Ribeiro, A. E., *Dress in Eighteenth Century Europe 1715–1789*, London 1984

Rudé, G., *The Crowd in the French Revolution*, Oxford 1959

— *Revolutionary Europe 1783–1815*, London 1964

Soboul, A., *The Parisian Sans-Culottes and the French Revolution 1793–4*, trans. G. Lewis, Oxford 1964

Stewart, J. H., *A Documentary Survey of the French Revolution*, New York 1951

Tannahill, R., *Paris in the Revolution*, London 1966

Thompson, J. M. (ed.), *English Witnesses of the French Revolution*, Oxford 1938

Twiss, R., *A Trip to Paris in July and August 1792*, Dublin 1793

Walter, G., *La Révolution française vue par ses journaux*, Paris 1948

Williams, H. M., *Letters from France*, ed. & intr. J. M. Todd, New York, 2 vols, 1975

Periodicals

Cabinet des Modes, later *Magasin des Modes Nouvelles Françaises et Anglaises*, 1785–9

Chronique de Paris 1789–93

Journal des Dames et des Modes 1797–1800

Journal de la Mode et du Goût 1790–93

Tableau General du Goût, des Modes et Costumes de Paris, 1797–9

Articles

Delpierre, M., 'A propos d'un manteau de représentant du peuple de 1798 récemment offert au Musée du Costume', in *Bulletin du Musée Carnavalet*, 1972, No. 1

Dowd, D. L., 'Jacobinism and the Fine Arts', in *Art Quarterly*, Detroit Institute of Arts, XVI, 1953

— 'The French Revolution and the Painters', in *French Historical Studies*, North Carolina State College, Vol. 1, No. 2, 1959

Harris, J., 'The Red Cap of Liberty: A Study of Dress Worn by French Revolutionary Partisans 1789–1794', in *Eighteenth-Century Studies*, University of California, Spring 1981

Mackrell, A., 'The Dress of the Parisian Élégantes with special reference to the Journal des Dames et des Modes from June 1797 until December 1799', MA Report, Courtauld Institute of Art, University of London 1977

Index

Note: Figures in italic type refer to pages on which illustrations appear.